POST-PANDEMIC PROFITS

Keys to Thriving in the Face of Adversity

POST-PANDEMIC PROFITS
Keys to Thriving in the Face of Adversity

Featuring:

Kevin Rogers

Brian Kurtz

Oscar Calderon

Mark Imperial

Tega Diegbe

Earl Flormata

Brennan Hopkins

Keita Hopkinson

Ryan Hunter

Pedro Meneses

Ben Stocks

Scott Sylvan Bell

Mark Tandan

Remarkable Press™

Royalties from the retail sales of **"POST-PANDEMIC PROFITS: Keys to Thriving in the Face of Adversity"** are donated to the Global Autism Project:

AUTISM KNOWS NO BORDERS;
FORTUNATELY NEITHER DO WE.®

The Global Autism Project 501(C)3, is a nonprofit organization which provides training to local individuals in evidence-based practice for individuals with autism.

The Global Autism Project believes that every child has the ability to learn and their potential should not be limited by geographical bounds.

The Global Autism Project seeks to eliminate the disparity in service provision seen around the world by providing high-quality training to individuals providing services in their local community. This training is made sustainable through regular training trips and contiguous remote training.

You can learn more about the Global Autism Project by visiting **GlobalAutismProject.org**

Copyright © 2020 Remarkable Press™

All rights reserved. No part of this publication may be reproduced, distributed or transmitted in any form or by any means, including photocopying, re-cording, or other electronic or mechanical methods, without the prior written, dated and signed permission of the authors and publisher, except as provided by the United States of America copyright law.

The information presented in this book represents the views of the author as of the date of publication. The author reserves the rights to alter and update their opinions based on new conditions. This book is for informational purposes only.

The author and the publisher do not accept any responsibilities for any liabilities resulting from the use of this information. While every attempt has been made to verify the information provided here, the author and the publisher cannot assume any responsibility for errors, inaccuracies or omissions. Any similarities with people or facts are unintentional.

Post-Pandemic Profits —1st ed.

Managing Editor/ Shannon Buritz

ISBN-13: 978-1-7323763-7-3

TABLE OF CONTENTS

A NOTE TO THE READER

Thank you for buying your copy of "POST-PANDEMIC PROFITS: Keys to Thriving in the Face of Adversity." This book was originally created as a series of live interviews, that's why it reads like a series of conversations, rather than a traditional book that talks at you.

I wanted you to feel as though the participants and I are talking with you, much like a close friend, or relative, and felt that creating the material this way would make it easier for you to grasp the topics and put them to use quickly, rather than wading through hundreds of pages.

So relax, grab a pen and paper, take notes and get ready to learn some fascinating strategies for achieving "Post-Pandemic Profits."

Warmest regards,

Mark Imperial
Publisher, Author and Radio Personality

INTRODUCTION

"POST-PANDEMIC PROFITS: Keys to Thriving in the Face of Adversity" is a collaborative book series featuring leading business growth experts. Get valuable advice from this round table discussion with an elite panel including: Kevin Rogers, Brian Kurtz, Oscar Calderon, Mark Imperial, Tega Diegbe, Earl Flormata, Brennan Hopkins, Keita Hopkinson, Ryan Hunter, Pedro Meneses, Ben Stocks, Scott Sylvan Bell and Mark Tandan.

Remarkable Press™ would like to extend a heartfelt thank you to all participants who took the time to submit their chapter and offer their support in becoming ambassadors for this project.

100% of the royalties from the retail sales of this book will be donated to the Global Autism Project. Should you want to make a direct donation, visit their website at: GlobalAutismProject.org

Kevin Rogers

Conversation with Kevin Rogers

Oscar Calderon: Hey everybody! This is Oscar Calderon AKA Rasco AKA Wolfman Jack. I'm here with Kevin Rogers. How are you doing, Kevin?

Kevin Rogers: Good, Oscar. Good to see you, brother. Love that beard. I'm jealous.

Oscar Calderon: Appreciate it. Kevin is the founder of Copy Chief along with being just a bad ass all around marketer. So I'm excited for this 10 minutes. Let's get it going. Kevin, tell us who you are, what you do and why we should listen to you?

Kevin Rogers: I'm Kevin Rogers and I spent 10 years of my life as a standup comedian in my twenties. That was a great time and turned out to be, more importantly, the foundation for a career as a copywriter. That means I write primarily direct response ads that are judged upon their ability to get a reader or a viewer of a video to take action at the end of it.

Oscar Calderson: Awesome. I love it. So with that said, what is the one thing we're going to talk about right now?

Kevin Rogers: The one thing I think about local businesses is that you have the power of being part of a community. And that's an advantage because people want to support you. I know I want to support my local businesses. It's killing me now that I can't go to businesses that I love to frequent. I think about the ones that I cared the most about. I know their origin story, why they exist and what they do that is special. And I think the simple job from a marketing standpoint of any business is to tell people what you do. What are you uniquely good at? And why are you uniquely qualified to deliver a special experience to a customer? Why can you offer the lowest price? Why can you give the best white glove service? Wherever you are on that spectrum, you opened the business because you saw a gap in the market. It's really important that you communicate that.

Oscar Calderson: Awesome. Why is it important for local business owners to target that in their messaging?

Kevin Rogers: I have a little formula that I created called the "rebel yell". The reason I call it that is because most local businesses in entrepreneurial endeavors are born of a rebellion, right? We don't fit it. Nobody would open and go through all the heartache of running their own business if they were comfortable showing up somewhere to get a paycheck. They would just do that. We're cursed with this desire for something better, something different for ourselves and our customers. So I came up with a two sentence framework that helps you capture that spirit of rebellion in a really simple "fill in the blank" format. . So if you want, I'll just read it and anybody watching or reading can write it down. I also have this for free on my website and a blog post. And I can tell you where to go if you need that, but I'll show it to you and then I'll give you some famous examples. Okay. So very simply, the statement goes like this: “My name is _____. I love _____, but was fed up with _____. So I created _____ that _____.” Okay. Two key words in there that are important to notice are “love” and “fed up” because those are powerful and motivating emotions. They are simple words that we use all the time, but how often do we think of a local business and know what they love? What is their passion and why did they open this business? Was it a life’s calling? And why were they fed up? What did they want to make better out of their own frustration and what do they want their customers to experience?

So here's how it would sound with some famous examples. See if you recognize this one. “My name is Steve. I love computers, but was fed up with the snail's pace of commercial technology. So I created a user-friendly computer that processes information faster than anything else out there today.” That’s Steve Jobs. And you want that computer. How about this one for an airline? “My name is Richard. I love to travel, but was fed up with lousy, expensive and unreliable airline travel. So I created an airline with competitive fares that arrives on time and treats every passenger with first class service.” That would be Virgin Airlines, right? So, most people know about Dollar Shave Club and they have a great viral video that kicked it off. “My name is Mike. I love a clean shave, but was fed up with paying through the nose for razors. So I created a simple subscription service that delivers quality razors right to your door for $1 a month.” So you can see when you fill in the blanks, it gets pretty interesting. And that's the heart of your story. And imagine if everybody who came into your business could leave knowing your story, how much more likely they would be to come back and bring friends next time.

Oscar Calderon: Wow. Yeah. And it gets straight to the point, right? This is how I am different from everyone else and this is what I have to offer because of that. It’s so simple, yet so powerful.

Kevin Rogers: Right. That's what I love about it, man. The hardest part about writing copy for ourselves is that we have so much to tell and want to tell it all. It's really hard to cut out everything else. And this forces you to do that. So I love templates like this. It's like everything you need to say, and if you just stick to it, you're like "Ohhh...this actually works."

Oscar Calderon: And once you have this in place, now your job is to spread it everywhere through your messaging, right?

Kevin Rogers: Yeah. And you can even expand on it. I have another thing called the 60 second sales hook. This is a four part storytelling mechanism. It consists of identity, struggle, discovery and result. It is very similar to the "rebel yell", but expanded a little. The keywords there are "struggle" and "discovery". When you are willing to share a struggle, that is a very human thing to do. Many big businesses aren't very good at that. They have learned to manufacture it and agencies have gotten better at getting that across, but it's rare that we feel the heart of a business. As entrepreneurs, that's our advantage. We don't have to hold a board meeting or meet with our lawyers to decide if we want to be honest about what motivated us to have a change in our lives, you know? So you say "I had this struggle that you can probably relate to, I discovered this way to fix it and now I'd like to share it with you." And that's it. The cool thing about it is you are not trying to be for everybody. You are simply defining who YOU are. And if people can relate to you, then you have something for them that they are going to love. If people think you're an idiot or couldn't possibly have a similar struggle, they can move on and find somebody different.

Oscar Calderon: I love it. The "struggle" part is what the bigger businesses are not doing. And you don't want to do business with a faceless company. You would rather do it with someone that you connect emotionally with. This part expands upon that vulnerability and emotional connection.

Kevin Rogers: Yeah. There has been a cool example recently. I don't know if you've seen this, but Domino's Pizza started running a campaign that basically says "Hey, our pizza sucked for awhile." I think the campaign is just great. They were like "We had some problems and our pizza didn't taste that good. We were delivering them late.". And you know, the fact that they came out and admitted those things and then said they have made changes, made me want to order Dominoes for the first time in 20 years to see if they were living up to their promise. But it really got my attention because in a rare case, they shared their struggle honestly and transparently and it really connects.

Oscar Calderson: Wow. Yeah. And that's what we all want. Right? We want an emotional connection, especially nowadays.

Kevin Rogers: Yeah. We demand it now because that's all we get. We are on social media like Facebook. We are used to knowing everything about every person we know. It's almost weird when someone doesn't have a Facebook account. How many friends do you have that don't have Facebook accounts? I can think of only two or three. It's interesting. It stands out now if we can't check on people we know. And so if every other way that people communicate involves that kind of transparency and you're trying to be secretive still, it's not going to connect.

Oscar Calderon: Wow. Love it. And this is how you stand out. I love it, Kevin. Thank you for all of this. This is really valuable and I'm sure it is going to help a lot of people. You mentioned a free resource. If people want to know more about you and what we have talked about, where can they go?

Kevin Rogers: Go to copychief.com/rebel-yell. Or you can just Google "copy chief rebel yell" and it will come up right away. And again, this is free. The 60 second sales hook is there for free as well. Let me email you. And if you like what I'm sending you and you think it's helpful, stick around. And if not, you can unsubscribe and it was good knowing you.

Oscar Calderon: I love it, Kevin. Thank you so much for your time. We'll talk to you soon.

Kevin Rogers: My pleasure, man. Take care. Good luck.

Kevin Rogers

Kevin Rogers spent years traveling the country as a dead-broke stand-up comedian until he discovered how a simple joke formula could be used as a powerful marketing hook and began teaching it to marketers.

Kevin's unique background as a nightclub comic and in-the-trenches salesperson provide a rare spectrum of experience and ability. His greatest strength is teaching anyone to use the power of their own story to connect better with customers and compel them to take action.

Today Kevin is one of the most in-demand sales consultants online, working closely with high-volume information marketers, corporations and local brick and mortar businesses alike to turn around sluggish ad campaigns.Entrepreneurs and business owners all over the world have used Kevin's techniques to skyrocket their profits and grow their businesses at record pace.

Kevin is the Amazon best-selling author of The 60-Second Sales Hook and founder of Copy Chief, a thriving community of the world's top online marketers.

WEBSITE: copychief.com/rebel-yell

Brian Kurtz

Conversation with Brian Kurtz

Oscar Calderon: Hey everybody. I am Oscar Calderon, AKA Racso. I'm being joined by a direct response marketing legend, Brian Kurtz. How are you doing, Brian?

Brian Kurtz: Good, good. I don't know if I'm a legend or not, but I'm totally quarantined, so I'm a quarantined legend if I'm a legend. It's good to be on Zoom since we can still talk on Zoom and it's nice to meet you.

Oscar Calderon: Nice to meet you too. Brian helped a three million dollar company go all the way to $150,000,000+ around the 2000s. His advertisements have been seen by over a billion people. So Brian might know a little bit about advertising and growing a business.

Brian Kurtz: I didn't do it alone and I did it with some of the best copywriters, so they made me look good. I was involved and committed, but I didn't do it myself by any means.

Oscar Calderon: All right, Brian. So we have 10 minutes. Let's dig in. Please tell us who you are, what you do, and why we should listen to you.

Brian Kurtz: For 34 years, I ran Boardroom. Then the last five or six I've been the owner of Titans Marketing, which is a direct marketing educational company. I've got two masterminds. I sell classic books like Gene Schwartz' "Breakthrough Advertising" and swipe files from great copywriters. Jay Abraham said to me a long time ago that if you did it, you have a responsibility or a moral obligation to teach it. And that's where I am right now. I'm teaching what I've learned. I'm also a student in that I go to rooms where I'm not the smartest person and I can learn from other people and then share what I know. And I guess the reason why people should listen to me is not just because of that, but because I have 40 years of experience. And it's not one year for 40 years. It's 40 years of cumulative experience by learning from the best of the best. And I think that's why people should listen to me because I have the accumulated knowledge in my head of some of the greatest mentors and greatest thinkers. I've had a good career. And it's something that gives me an opportunity to share wisdom. When I was starting out at 23 years old, most of the people I looked up to were the 60, 70 and 80 year olds who had all the wisdom and now most of them are dead. So I have to carry on the torch for them.

Oscar Calderon: Awesome. I can't wait to dig in because I'm sure we're going to learn a lot of things from all those years in the business. So with that said, what is the one thing we're going to talk about today?

Brian Kurtz: So I'm going to give you an umbrella topic, which is "messaging during Covid". Then I'm going to talk about two specific types of industries that can take that idea and run with it. So the "messaging" message I want to leave you with is that you can't be tone deaf to what's going on and you also don't have to make it your point of emphasis in every email or every time you talk to somebody. I'm sure you've heard this before from some of your other speakers. And what I mean by "don't be tone deaf", is that everybody knows that we're in a pandemic. It's the conversation that's going on in their brain, but you don't have to beat them home with it. You don't need a subject line that says "Cures for Covid", or "The best things you can do for Covid" or "Coronavirus" or "Pandemic". So I think what you need to do is just touch that message in their head or just remind them. The two ideas I have are for restaurants and doctors or practitioners who see people in offices.

When I think about restaurants, I don't want them to have a Covid strategy. I want them to do things such as an idea I got from Frank Kern, like dialing up every single college student or high school student to become their pony express for delivery. Because you can deliver or you can have people pick up. But take it a step further and there's an element of direct mail you can put into this too. Because I've been home for six weeks, I haven't gotten one menu from a restaurant that is open for delivery or for pickup. I'm wondering why that is because I used to always get menus in my mailbox. And I remember when I lived in an apartment, there were menus all over the floor of the lobby. So why am I not getting menus? So I don't think that they should use the college students for delivery first. Use them for menu distribution and not just the regular menu. I think they need a menu that emphasizes the thought that's going on in their head about Covid without saying Covid. So how would I do that? I would take those college students and have them go door to door in my restaurant area. I would have them drop off a flier that basically says "I want to cook dinner for you tonight" and have it signed by the restaurant owner. And then you highlight the key items that you're famous for in that restaurant. So you have like three or four items and you say at the bottom "call this number". The whole concept is "I'm open. You're stuck. I've got the food for you." After you do that, you can hopefully get the phone numbers. It's all local. And so you just go out and be proactive. That's the key point here. You are proactive with the students, the direct mail and the phone calls. Drop off the special menu and then call and ask if they received it and what night they would like to have you cook for them. So that's my overall idea for restaurants. It takes into account that the ones who are going to be proactive are the ones that are going to get much more business than the ones who are sitting back. I mean, they might have a sign outside the restaurant that says "We're open for delivery or curbside pickup", but this takes it a step further.

Then there are the people that have a patient driven business. We'll say a chiropractor, a gym or a physical therapy practice. You can't just stop doing business. In the case of a chiropractor I have as a

client, I said "You're patients can't come see you. So what are you going to do?"
It's the concept that you don't have to make everything. You can buy some of it. So if you don't sell pain supplements in your office, drop ship from somebody you can make a deal with. It could be anything from supplements to pain lasers. Then you go to your patients and say "You're stuck at home. I'm stuck in my office. I wanted to find some things that could help you before you can come and see me again. Here's some stuff for you." And you sell them that. You can take a piece of it. You might not want to take a piece of it. Sell it to them at cost and then give them a path to the future once they are out of the house. Offer a free visit once they can return to the office.

On the other hand, the guy who's got the physical therapy, acupuncture or meditation practice, can do telehealth. Give clients a solid message that says "You're stuck at home. My best therapists and fitness trainers and meditation experts are all stuck at home too. Let's bring you guys together. We've got telehealth for you." You give them a couple free or discounted sessions and then they may start paying for it. But even if they don't, you overdeliver on everything you've got. The key is to put them in the offices when things are better. And ultimately it's all about overdelivering. I'm not trying to make the Coronavirus into a small thing. It is a big thing, but while it's happening, you've got opportunities to give away more than you ever have before. Then people will hopefully remember when they are out of their houses and can visit you again. They will have more loyalty to you if you deliver a great product or service in the meantime.

Oscar Calderon: I love it. And this creates a sense of reciprocity for the consumer. So now they want to do business with you.

Brian Kurtz: It does. You can't bank on reciprocity. You have to overdeliver with the notion that I'm doing it because I care about you as a patient or client. And you don't even say that I'm doing this because I hope you come into my office. It's kind of a built in reciprocity. If they don't do it, you can't hold it against them. A lot of people will and you just hope for that scenario.

Oscar Calderon: Right. I love it. And also like you said, being tone deaf about all of this, you have to acknowledge where we are right now. You don't have to make it the point of every conversation, but just start with "this is where we are right now and this is what I have for you."

Brian Kurtz: Right. Under the circumstances, I came up with the solution of taking my amazing meditation instructors, putting them on Zoom with you and having a great session together. Try to do this affordably or free. A lot of live events are being offered virtually now and they are selling tickets as if it is a real event. I have a mastermind group,and if I can't hold the event in September, I'll do it virtually. I don't think I will count it toward their membership. I'm going to give them a really good event and extend their membership out because I can afford to and I want to, but you don't have to. That's up to the individual. But whatever it is, you want to be over delivering.

Oscar Calderon: One hundred percent. I just wanted to touch on what you mentioned about drop shipping. It could be a high perceived value item that's low cost, right? So it doesn't break the bank. That would be the perfect balance for it.

Brian Kurtz: Yeah. And if you can do a high price item and if you think your customers would pay for it, you can just do it at cost. Basically say "I'm going to get you a thousand dollar laser that costs $500 and I'm not taking anything for it. Or you can go the other way, sell it to them for $1,000 and take whatever you get out of that. But you can do it either way. You don't want to take a loss, but doing it at cost can be a great way to do it. And you're right. You can do small things that have high perceived value.

Oscar Calderon: I love it. Ryan, thank you so much for this. We did 12 minutes and 29 seconds. All good.

Brian Kurtz: Good. I didn't know if I was going over it, so that's good.

Oscar Calderon: That was amazing. Thank you so much for all the good ideas that you gave us and I'm sure that if people implement them, this will be very helpful. This is money in their pockets, so thank you for that. And if people want to know more about you and what you do, where can they find you?

Brian Kurtz: If they want to spend $17 on my book, they can go to overdeliverbook.com and they get an amazing bonus package that's worth thousands of dollars. I've got Jay Abraham stuff on there, Dan Kennedy, Gary Bencivenga and Perry Marshall. It's just great, great material. And so they go to overdeliverbook.com and they get on my list. I don't do affiliates. I just send content every week and they buy my book on Amazon or wherever and they come back to the site and get all these bonuses for free. If they don't want to spend $17 and just want to get free content and be on my list and learn more about me, they can go to briankurtz.net and can opt in and get lots of free content and all sorts of stuff on my site that they might really enjoy. So that's how they can get in touch with me.

Oscar Calderon: Alright, awesome Brian. Brian literally wrote the book on overdelivering.

Brian Kurtz: I did. And the funny thing was the book was called "Overdeliver". So I had to over deliver on the bonus page. I guarantee even if you don't buy the book, go to overdeliverbook.com and just see what I'm giving away to buy a $17 book. I think you'll be amazed.

Oscar Calderon: Brian, thank you so much. I appreciate your time and we'll be in touch.

Brian Kurtz: Thank you.

BRIAN KURTZ

Titans Marketing

Brian Kurtz has had two careers.

The first spanned 34 years as a force behind Boardroom Inc., an iconic publisher and direct marketer.

During that time, he was mentored by, and worked with, a who's who of marketing legends (who he owes everything to).

And more specifically, he worked side-by-side with the most prolific copywriters who have ever lived.

His second career, which he is five years into as the Founder of Titans Marketing, is a direct marketing educational and coaching company where he has also continued working with the best-of-the-best.

Titans Marketing is currently known for two mastermind groups, one serving top direct marketers, Titans Mastermind, and one serving a much wider group including the top up-and-comers in the industry, Titans Xcelerator.

He also has the exclusive rights to an array of classic books (such as Breakthrough Advertising) and swipe files Brian has re-published and created from notable copywriters such as Bill Jayme and Jim Rutz.

He is the author of two books himself.

His most recent book is Overdeliver: Build a Business for a Lifetime Playing the Long Game in Direct Response Marketing. It is his opus and comes with incredible bonuses at www.OverdeliverBook.com.

His first book, The Advertising Solution, profiles six legends of advertising and copywriting including Gene Schwartz, David Ogilvy and Gary Halbert. It can be found with fantastic bonuses as well at www.TheLegendsBook.com.

As a business-to-consumer marketer at Boardroom, Brian was responsible for selling over a billion dollars' worth of products "$39 at a time" to millions.

As a business-to-business marketer with Titans Marketing, he has sold over $6 million worth of products (and services) to thousands, enabling them to spread the gospel about direct marketing to millions.

During both careers, he has been a serial direct marketer, with a foundation in the eternal truths and fundamentals of direct response…while being committed to “overdelivering” over almost four decades.

WEBSITE: www.briankurtz.net and www.OverdeliverBook.com

Oscar Calderon

The Promotional Pentagon

5 Steps to Turning Bad Ads into Good Ads

By: Oscar Calderon

"Stopping advertising to save money is like stopping your watch to save time." – Henry Ford

Alright, Mr. Ford, we get it. Problem is, for most of us mortals, advertising can look like a scary monster whose only purpose is to empty our bank accounts. Been there, done that, am I right? Yet, it really doesn't have to be that way.

I'm here to tell you that you don't have to burn a hole in your pocket every time you run a promotion or pray to the universe hoping your ads work at least this one time. In fact, you don't even need a ridiculous amount of money to start running ads.

Truth is: You can start small and then scale up - AFTER you find a winning, working, and profitable ad, of course.

So, let's dive in, shall we?

I'm about to simplify your current advertising process into digestible chunks even my grandma can chew - so that your promotions finally resonate with your target audience… so that your promotions finally generate the response you really wanted... so that your promotions build your brand while simultaneously putting cash into your little pockets.

Direct Response Advertising vs Brand Advertising

In a nutshell, Direct Response advertising measures the success of each campaign by how many responses it generates. It's all about getting your customers to TAKE ACTION. Whether that is to fill out a survey, come to your store, call you, enter their contact information, or get them to do handstands *(if that's what your ad was pushing for).*

Direct Response advertising *physically* moves your target audience into taking the action you want them to take. Unlike branding, it's NOT about cutesy slogans, artistic graphics, getting awards, stroking your ego, or impressing your family, friends, and investors.

With Direct Response advertising, you're able to track the response your ads generate down to the last cent. This way, you have tangible numbers that show you whether you should keep your ad, tweak it, or start fresh. You MUST keep track of your numbers though, otherwise, you could end up trashing an ad that was performing well… or worse, keep running one that's eating your money away.

Once you have a proven campaign, advertising is NOT a gamble anymore - but a systematic, duplicatable, replicable process that generates RESULTS. Instead of hoping and trying your luck with *'spray and pray'* campaigns, you now have a fine-tuned money-making machine that multiplies your dollars indefinitely and at will.

Have some urgent bills suddenly show up? Need to pay your staff? Wanna take a vacation? Turn on that proven campaign and start counting the money coming your way. The key here is you MUST be proactive in getting and attracting clients your way. *(Note: I didn't say chase… but ATTRACT).*

After that, you turn your attention into nurturing them periodically, reminding them every once in a while about you and your offers, and getting them to come back over and over again. To do this, you must stay in constant communication with your audience to achieve that *'know, like, and trust'* factor- and *'top-of-mind'* awareness.

Be careful, though. You gotta be aware of what Dan Kennedy calls *"being an annoying pest vs being a welcomed guest."* You don't just want to be making a bunch of desperate offers that make you look like an obnoxious used-car salesman. That's how you lose business.

Instead, you need to be relevant to your clients' needs, empathizing with their problems and helping them reach their goals. In other words, ***becoming their trusted advisor <u>even before</u> money exchanges hands***.

Sadly, most schools don't teach this. Which means, most businesses' ads look the same. One look at the Yellow Pages, your local newspaper, or billboards around your city and you will notice this reality.

One thing to always remember is: People love to buy - they just hate being sold to.

With that said, let's dig in! I'm about to break down the Promotional Pentagon so that your next ads become less of a gamble and more of a proven process you can replicate at will.

The first element of the Promotional Pentagon is:

PERCOLATE

You know, preparing, planning and plotting your campaigns ahead of time. How do you do this? Simply by aligning 3 specific KEY elements I like to call the Transactional Trifecta *(inspired by Dan Kennedy's Marketing Triangle)*. And they are:

Your Peeps - Your Promos - Your Pathways

Get this trifecta right and you'll be closer to a winning campaign than ever before. And by 'winning' I mean generating multiples of them Benjamins. So, let's break it down:

Your Peeps - Determine who your current best customers *(aka Premium Players)* are. Who has bought from you in the last 30-60-90 days? Who has bought from you repeatedly during that chosen time period? Who has spent the most money with you during your chosen time-frame?

Audit your own list of prospects and clients and see which characteristics they all share with one another. Why? Because *'birds of a feather flock together'*. Meaning, your Premium Players will, most likely, be friends with others like them. As in, they'll refer and recommend you to people who are like them. Plus, when you do business with your Premium Players who know, like and trust you, it's just more fun.

Your Promos - This relates to the messaging and offers your campaign contains. Now that you have selected who your Premium Players are, you can market EXCLUSIVELY to them.

"But, aren't we neglecting others by only focusing on a small pocket of people?"

Yes! One. Hundred. Percent. In fact, that's EXACTLY what you want. Listen, if you try to talk to everyone, your message won't resonate *fully* with anyone. You need to come up with a specific offer that only speaks to your Premium Players. After all, they're BUYERS who spend money in your business on a consistent basis. **Don't be afraid to repel non-buyers...** ***they don't pay your bills!***

Your Pathways - This relates to your distribution channels. Meaning, what avenues will you use to reach your Premium Players? Ask yourself: *"What do my Premium Players read? What do they watch? What other products or services do they buy? Where do they live? How much money do they make?"* With this information, you'll know exactly where to hit them. And which distribution channels generate the best result.

Here's a quick example of what I mean:

Joe Polish tells a story where a carpet cleaning service provider client of his comes to him *angrily* complaining that his ads are not working and he's been losing money. Joe asks to see the ad and to show him where he was sending it. It turns out the ad was a direct mail piece being sent to a *specific* zip code in order to get carpet cleaning clients.

Curious as to what was really happening, Mr Joe Polish gets into his car to see where exactly the letters were being sent. What happened next left Joe speechless...

It wasn't the advertisement. It wasn't the messaging in the letter. It was the fact that the letters were being sent to a neighborhood where people lived in rented apartments. **The whole campaign was being sent to the WRONG target market.**

When it comes to the Transactional Trifecta, this carpet cleaner had only one thing right. While this guy might have had the right Pathway *(direct mail)*, his targeting of the right Peeps was way off *(he needed people who owned homes NOT rented apartments)*, which then by default meant his Promo was off *(cuz the messaging was meant for owners or landlords, NOT renters).*

With the Transactional Trifecta your ads and messaging get higher response since the messaging fits the specific target audience through the right avenues ;)

The next element in the Promotional Pentagon is:

PENETRATE

The fastest way to get your advertising campaigns to resonate with your prospects and clients is to enter the conversation currently happening in their minds.

How do you do this? By interviewing your buyers and asking them WHY they buy from you. By having conversations with your prospects and finding out why they're still on the fence. By taking a look at the marketplace and seeing what messaging your competitors are using *(so that you hit your Premium Players from another angle)*. By reading your own best AND worst reviews. And finally, by going over your competitors' reviews and feedback.

Once you know your Premium Players like the back of your hand, including their fears, pains, worries, frustrations, complaints, goals, desires, aspirations, and dreams, you can tailor your messaging to hit them right where it counts. Your goal is to help them reach *their* goals.

Now, this is the perfect time to create your Proprietary Proclamation. This is your point of differentiation, as in what makes YOU unique and how you stand out. Whether that is being the cheapest, the fastest, the best quality, etc. What hole in your marketplace are your competitors not fulfilling? Or perhaps, what are your competitors not sharing about the product or service your Premium Players love?

For example, there was a story about Claude Hopkins *(a badass marketer/copywriter back in the day*) who was hired to create an ad about Schlitz beer. *"Schlitz beer"*, you say? Yes, way back when it was a thing.

Claude Hopkins went to the brewery, walked through the process, sampled the product and was tasked to write a campaign promoting the beer. During his visit, Mr Hopkins asked about the process of filtration but was told not to pay attention to it as it was the same as all the beers out there. No differentiation at all.

But guess what? **No one** knew about the filtration process.

Claude Hopkins knew that beer-drinkers and buyers didn't know how beer was made because no other beer companies were highlighting their process. So what did he do? He broke down the process inside the ad step by step.

And it took Schlitz beer from unknown to #2 in the US during that period of time.

Other examples of a successful Proprietary Proclamation: Geico's *'15 minutes could save you 15% or more in car insurance'*. Domino's *'Fresh pizza delivered to you in 30 minutes or your money back'*. Hertz' *'We're number 2 so we try harder'*.

Whether it's unique by you only or no one knows about it, this is how you penetrate your marketplace successfully.

Remember, the more you can articulate your Premium Players' problems better than they can themselves, the more they'll know you know your sh*t. This helps with positioning your product or service specifically to them, that it sells itself *with relative ease.*

It's now time to craft your messaging with the next element of the Promotional Pentagon...

PERSUADE

Now that you've done some planning and targeted research, it's time to actually put pen to paper. You know, crafting your next promotion into a guaranteed sale.

Here are a handful of proven mechanisms *(or Conversion Levers)* to make your next promotion that much more enticing, engaging, and compelling:

Conversion Lever #1: WIIFM ("What's in it for me?") - Here's a truth bomb: Your customers don't really care how long you've been in business... where you went to school... what kind of slogan you have... or whether your ad looks artistic or not...

They care about what YOU can do for THEM. As in, how you can SOLVE their PROBLEM. And everything related to -you guessed it- them. So use that; appeal to their self-interest. Give them the benefits of your product or service in great detail. Make them realize how your product or service will better their lives.

Conversion Lever #2: Reason Why - We, as human beings, are skeptical. Always looking for "what's the catch?". If they smell BS from a mile away *(even if what you're saying is 100% true)*, they're gone. Forever. So let them know why your products are being discounted. Let them know why you're offering them such a crazy deal. Fill them in. Give them a reason - no matter what that is. That way you'll ease up their skepticism, which will lead them to the sale MUCH more easily.

Conversion Lever #3: Anticipate objections - Address your clients' objections before they appear and you'll have a smoother path to the sale. *(Which is much, much easier now since you already hit the 'Percolate' and 'Penetrate' components of the Promotional Pentagon!)*

Conversion Lever #4: Storytelling - Give them a glimpse behind the scenes. Let them see the real you. Tell stories about your business, your staff and how your products came to be. No one likes to do business with a faceless company. Humans *crave* that connection.

Conversion Lever #5: Show, don't tell - *"A picture is worth a thousand words"*. Showcase your knowledge, skills, and talents in a way that's relevant to your audience. In other words, in a way that helps them reach their goals.

Conversion lever # 6: Proof - Make your argument stronger with statistics, facts, and proven research. Also, make sure you use testimonials and case studies from people who are just like your Premium Players. So they can see themselves achieving their goals, too - just like your past clients have. Use *'before and after'* pictures. Borrow credibility from leaders who your audience knows and follows. This way, you're letting them know your product or service WORKS.

Conversion Lever #7: CTA - Always have a *'call to action'*. Whether that is to come to your store, leave their contact information, bring a coupon, call you, or refer a friend. Make sure you lead your audience into doing what you want them to do. Otherwise, no one's going to do anything and you'll lose sales because of it, obvs.

Conversion Lever #8: Urgency and scarcity - Have a deadline or limit the amount of stock you're willing to sell. This helps push fence-sitters into action. Remind them your offer is ending when it reaches a specific date or time. But make sure to follow through - or they'll smell your BS from a mile away and never believe you again.

Conversion Lever #9: Risk reversal - Take the risk off your audience's shoulders and put them on your own. You'll be shocked by how this increases your response and conversions. The easier the path to the sale, the more sales you'll get. This also shows them you really believe in your own product or service. That's why you're giving them a 30-60-90 day guarantee. That's why you have no problem providing them a 'money back' promise. Because you *wholeheartedly* believe you can help them.

Now that you have your promotion ready to go, it's time for the next element of the Promotional Pentagon:

PROPAGATE

Spread the word. Share your message. Test your ads against each other. Track response down to the last cent. Tweak based on winning feedback and optimize. Because not ALL your promotions are gonna be a homerun from the get-go.

Your Premium Players will dictate whether you have a winning promotion or not by handing you their hard-earned cash and throwing it at your face to get your deliverables. They vote with their money. And THAT'S the only measurement of success you need.

With that said, based on the frequency of your promotions, your ads will fatigue at some point. Meaning, their selling power will go down as more people see it. That's why it's a good rule of thumb to test different angles, themes, headlines, and offers, as well as different Conversion Levers against each other *constantly*.

By the way, once you find your winning promotion *(or "control")*, you have an ASSET you can use and deploy *indefinitely*. Which means you can "turn it on and off" at will - whenever you need some urgent cash.

Once you find your winning promotion, you can also REPURPOSE your content in other avenues. Like so:

Blog posts can be turned into podcasts. Podcasts can be turned into videos. Videos can be turned into ebooks. Ebooks can be turned into audio. You can turn internal data into case studies. Use testimonials, statistics, reviews into content. Among other things.

This way, you and your brand create that *'omnipresent'* effect and you become UNDENIABLE. In fact, it's your DUTY to do everything and anything possible to put your deliverables in their faces. Because, if you don't, you're doing your audience a disservice. By letting them go to a competitor who won't treat them as well as you do - or by leaving them alone trying to figure it out on their own. So, it's not only in your best interest but THEIR best interest to do business with you.

Remember: *"You have brilliance in you, your contribution is valuable, and the art you create is precious. Only you can do, and you must."* – Seth Godin

So, do ;)

The final piece of the Promotional Pentagon is:

PERPETUATE

If you want to reach more people, sell more products, and/or keep the cash flow coming in, you need to turn your promotions on *regularly*. And by promotions, I don't just mean ads and paid campaigns. I mean being in constant communication with your audience. To keep that *'top of mind'* effect. To remain indoctrinating your peeps into your methodology. To deepen that connection you have going on with them. To develop that *'know, like, and trust'* factor.

Here's the thing, it costs 3 times more money to generate a NEW client from scratch than it costs to keep one. So your main goal here is to nurture your relationship with your audience. To keep them engaged and coming back for more.

On average, ask yourself how long your clients stay with you. How often do they come back to you? How much do they spend with you? With that number in your head, now you have a better idea of how much you can spend on your promotions.

Now, the avenue or medium you use to keep in contact with your audience is not that important. It could be emails, physical newsletters, postcards, social media, texts or videos. Just make sure it's somewhere your specific audience hangs out.

Also, *'train'* your audience to anticipate your communications, pick a medium and a schedule, and stick to it.

And, of course, don't forget to run birthday-and-holiday promotions! *(Just another excuse to hit them with more content and campaigns)*

With that said, make sure your communications are RELEVANT to them. Keep them engaged. Entertained. Because… ***boring kills the sale.***

That's it! Those are the 5 elements of the Promotional Pentagon. Use them and I'm sure you'll have a blast coming up with promotions and campaigns that actually work and bring you results. That is, for every dollar you put in, you get two or more in return!

Oscar Calderon

Oscar Calderon is a marketing consultant and self-proclaimed 'ad nerd'. He lives and breathes advertising and loves helping small business owners grow through simple yet tested marketing methods. Oscar's strategy focuses on client generation, client reactivation, and client retention. A student of the game, he loves testing new ideas and 'out of the box' angles to yield positive results - obsessing to connect ads to sales.

WEBSITE: adnerd.co

EMAIL: oscar@adnerd.co

Mark Imperial

Conversation with Mark Imperial

Oscar Calderon: Hey, everybody. I'm Oscar and I'm here with Mark Imperial. How's it going, Mark?

Mark Imperial: Hey! Good, Oscar. Great to be here.

Oscar Calderon: Mark is the creator and host of Remarkable Radio. He's also a digital owner and he's worked with amazing companies such as Nintendo and UFC. I'm really excited about this because I know I'm going to learn something and you guys are going to learn a lot in terms of marketing for local business owners. Mark, can you let us know in your own words, who you are and what you do?

Mark Imperial: Thanks, Oscar. I'm happy to be here and thanks for thinking of me. I'm a direct response marketing and sales advisor, as well as a publisher for entrepreneurs, professionals, and entire organizations that want an easy and fast way to stand out in a sea of competition.

Oscar Calderon: Perfect. Let's dig in. What is the one thing we are going to talk about today?

Mark Imperial: Well, I was thinking we should talk about the nucleus of everyone's marketing. Over the past 14 or 15 years, I've really boiled it down to one thing that you can do. It is the most effective thing you could work on because once you get this thing done, it becomes the nucleus of all of your marketing. And that is having a published book for yourself.

Oscar Calderon: I love it. Why is it important for business owners to have a published book?

Mark Imperial: First and foremost, it's a giant shortcut because in today's short attention span society, people are always looking for a fast way to size you up. You know, just like when you are at a social gathering, people are looking at each other and trying to figure out where they fit on the social ladder. Are they above me in status or below me? Who is this person? Our prospects are the same way. If you're in a sea of competition, people want to know, "Is this the person I should choose? Do they know their stuff? Do they understand my problem?" And one of the fastest ways to demonstrate that and to choose would be, "Hey, does this person have their own published book? Have they written the book on the subject where 99% of their competition likely has not?" So that's benefit number one...giving people a shortcut to immediately identify you as an obvious expert in your field and someone they want to work with. If we look at famous people like Dave Ramsey or Suze Orman, they have published books. The book kind of serves as their "wrapper." It defines them. It's an easy way for people to identify who they are and immediately telegraphs their subject matter or what their expertise is. So it's really about using a book to gain more publicity opportunities. Let's face it, I'm on the radio myself and whenever I'm looking for a subject matter expert in any field, the first people I look for are the ones who have written books. I can either say, "Hey, I was looking for somebody to talk about marketing and I found these people in the phone book”, or “My guest today is the author of ‘Direct Marketing Today’.” You know what I mean? It makes the interviewer look better as well. So it's always best to use it. Congruently, you can use a book to create speaking engagements. If you ever wanted to go out and speak on stages, you have a book to really lead with and say, “Hey, I'm the author of this book.” It will immediately get the attention of the promoter, chamber or organization over somebody that just walks in with a business card.

The list of benefits is really endless. How about referrals? If you want to get more referrals, having a book to pass off to your best clients is a great way to do it. Simply say “I really appreciate your business. If you have a family member or friend that could use my help, kindly give them a copy of my book”, and hand them a stack. Your referrals are the lifeblood of your business and the book does all of that positioning and pre-selling for you. Not to mention, what about referral partners? For example, are you an insurance company that relies on referrals from mortgage professionals? Give a stack of books to your mortgage partner that can hand them out to their clients. So it's really about getting referrals in so many different ways from your clients and other organizations.

Having a book also changes you from being just a salesperson to a trustworthy advisor. It's a total shift. It's not like, “Hey, buy my stuff.” It's more about, “What can I share with you that will help you in making your choices?” In addition, it leverages your time. A lot of people will say, “Hey, Mark, this isn’t important to me. I just don’t have the time to write a book. I’m too busy trying to sell my stuff.” But it’s actually the opposite. Think about it. It's not about how much time it is going to take you to create a book. It's about how much time it will save you once the book is done and all the repetitive yammering that you do when you talk to folks isn’t necessary anymore. The book will do all of that for you. So it really leverages your time. It can be out there like the perfect salesman soldier pre-selling for you while you're asleep. Those are just a handful of the benefits to having your own published book.

Oscar Calderon: One hundred percent. It's like a quiet, unpaid salesman working for you nonstop, right?

Mark Imperial: I love it. That's one of my favorite things about it. It works the same way as videos and other content that you can create.

Oscar Calderon: Give us a quick breakdown as to how anyone could start creating their book today.

Mark Imperial: Sure. Absolutely. We can definitely accomplish that. First and foremost, before I break down the steps for you, people may have hesitations about writing a book such as "I'm not a good writer. I can't write a book. That's not for me. I just don't have the confidence." In reality, if you are already selling your products or services by talking to people every day, whether you realize it or not, you're already writing a book. It's really about the content in your head that you express to people all the time about your subject matter. You are writing the book. The only thing you haven't done is collect that information and clone it in a book. Should I go ahead and break down the steps now?

Oscar Calderon: Please. I'm taking notes right now.

Mark Imperial: These books are essentially sales letters. You know a thing or two about sales letters, right, Oscar? They're essentially long form sales letters. You also can look at them like they mimic a one on one consultation with your ideal prospect. It allows readers to eavesdrop on that perfect consultation with that ideal prospect. And if they can put themselves in the shoes of that person that you're having the consultation with, they can say, "Yes, this is for me. This person can help me."

So let's go right into the steps. Step number one. Before you write your book, you have to decide...what is the objective of the book? What do you want it to achieve? People often overlook this. After someone reads your book, what do you want them to do? Are you trying to get a one on one consultation? So you can have a real meaningful sales opportunity and conversation with them? If that's what you want to do, we're going to write the book a specific way. Do you want to make a small sale? Are you trying to let this book sell a tripwire or entry level product of yours? We're going to write the book a certain way if that's the case. So step number one is coming up with the objective. What do you want it to achieve?

Step number two is making a list of what your ideal prospect needs to know from you in order to take that step or reach that objective. Just off the top of my head, a lot of people want to know, "Is this for me? Do you serve people like me?" You know, just like the old Dan Kennedy saying, "But my business is different." Everybody seems to think their problem is unique. Can you address that in the book? How are you going to demonstrate that what you have to offer is for everybody, regardless of their unique situation? And what is the risk for them to find out more? If it's just a complimentary consultation that you're offering, people want to know exactly what is going to happen to them if they reach out to you. Laying out the steps and how it's risk-free for them to find out more are important things to include in the book. Give the reader the information they need to reach the objective.

Step number three is organizing your content. You're going to create a framework or an outline, otherwise known as the table of contents. As I mentioned before, books are long form sales letters. You're going to use things like "frequently asked" questions. What are the top questions that people ask all the time and the answers to them. So you just need to write down the questions, right? What are the "should ask" questions? People often don't think about these questions. "Should ask" questions are questions that you want your prospect to have the answers to, but they might not have enough knowledge on the subject to even think to ask. When you can demonstrate that you have those steps, it also elevates your status as far as the obvious expert. The idea is that you give them enough to say yes, but not too little that they end up saying no. There is a fine line when it comes to length of content, just like sales copy.

Step number four is organizing your content. We can help you with this, or you can do it on your own. After you have written down all your notes and questions, you can start to answer those questions. I recommend recording your answers. If you have opted for us to help you with this step, you would book a content extraction call with us. In as little as 90 minutes to a couple of hours, we can get all the content out of your brain over the phone. Then we transcribe those answers and my writing team takes it from there. They listen to the way you speak and write the content "in your own voice."

Step five is a completely "hands off" process that my team takes care of for you. This involves book creation, editing, layout, formatting, cover design and publishing to all the major platforms including Amazon, Kindle and distribution through Barnes and Noble. After that, you're off to the races and ready to use this book every single day as the nucleus of your marketing.

For example, a client of mine in the mortgage business created a book with us entitled "Sold and Closed." He is a mortgage guy who is working on growing his own team. He also wants to start a coaching business, helping other mortgage professionals to increase their sales. So he wrote this book about "new school methods for growing your real estate or MLO business." It is aimed at the type of audience he wants to attract. It is a nice, easy read with a call to action at the end of each chapter. The end goal is to get the reader to book a phone call with him where he will interview them and find out if they are a good fit for his coaching program. Lo and behold, he will then make them an offer.

I want to make sure to mention that writing a book doesn't have to be scary. People have the misconception that you have to write so much and it will take so much time. We can literally get all of the content out of your head in that 90 minute to a couple of hours time frame. Most of our books are less than 100 pages. What we have found over the years, especially in today's "short attention span society", is that books are more likely to be read if they are easily and quickly digestible. Today, the brevity definitely counts. Amazon even has categories for books that can be read in 20-30 minutes or less because people want that. If you can give a book like that to potential clients and make it easy for them to consume, it draws them that much closer to you.

Oscar Calderon: It's one thing to have a book to give away, but another thing for the reader to actually go through it.

Mark Imperial: Absolutely. Another quick example is the book "Your Ultimate Wedding Reception." This book was written by a wedding entertainer who uses it at bridal shows and as a lead magnet on his website. He sends it to local media and gets phone calls such as, "Hey, we are doing a special segment for Valentine's Day on love and marriage. Can you talk?" And he can literally say, "Yes, I wrote the book on it!" That's how it works. It is such a simple, yet overlooked principle.

Oscar Calderon: It's powerful. Just like you said, being a book author gives you a status that propels you to the next level.

Mark Imperial: Instantly! In a matter of a couple hours invested time...instantly!

Oscar Calderon: Mark, if anyone is interested in writing a book or getting your help to do it "hands free", where can they find you?

Mark Imperial: They can go to booksgrowbusiness.com. I go into depth on each step that I described in this short amount of time. You can get that free training at booksgrowbusiness.com.

Oscar Calderon: Mark, you dropped some value bombs! I'm so excited. Thank you so much for this. Thank you for your time.

Mark Imperial: It's my pleasure, Oscar. Thanks so much for having me.

Mark Imperial

Mark Imperial is a Best Selling Author, Syndicated Business Columnist, Syndicated Radio Host, and internationally recognized Stage, Screen, and Radio Host of numerous business shows spotlighting leading experts, entrepreneurs, and business celebrities.

Mark got started in Marketing and Advertising to grow sales for his DJ Entertainment business. His effective methods for "Marketing Entertainment" drew the attention of big brands and he became the event marketing voice for some of the world's most loved brands, including UnderArmour, Nintendo, and M&M/Mars Candy, to name a few.

One day he looked up and realized his passion and gift had evolved from just Entertainment to growing brands by mixing Entertainment with Advertising, Direct Marketing, and Promotions.

In the years since then, Mark has immersed himself in Direct Marketing, learning from the best mentors, including the Legendary Dan Kennedy and founded several businesses helping Entrepreneurs and professionals in private practice become more successful.

Today, Mark focuses on helping businesses implement the most effective, measurable marketing by handling all the technical aspects for them.

WEBSITE: booksgrowbusiness.com , markimperial.com

EMAIL: mark@markimperial.com

Tega Diegbe

Conversation with Tega Diegbe

Oscar Calderon: Hey, everybody. I'm Oscar Calderon AKA Rasco. I'm being joined by Tega Diegbe. How's it going?

Tega Diegbe: Oh, he got it right! It's going good. How are you?

Oscar Calderon: I'm great. Thank you for being here. We're about to kill it in 10 minutes to talk about actionable tips, tactics and strategies that local business owners can use right now. So let's get it going! Please tell us who you are, what you do and why we should listen to you?

Tega Diegbe: My name is Tega Diegbe. I would be classed as an operations manager for a small and highly engaged entrepreneur community. In terms of the online stuff, I help put systems in place to make things run smoothly and make sure we deliver everything that we promise to customers. And then on the side, I have a very small Facebook ads agency, where we help local clients get business and customers through the door using Facebook ads.

Oscar Calderon: Awesome. Please tell us...what is the one thing we are going to talk about today?

Tega Diegbe: We are going to talk about how to reactivate some old customers and get them to either come back to your store or get them back in communication with you.

Oscar Calderon: Awesome. Why is that important for local business owners to do?

Tega Diegbe: I think it's important for them to do because then they are not spending all of their time trying to get new customers. What do they say? A bird in the hand is worth two in the bush, right? So the same thing applies. If you have somebody that has already spent money at your business, they know how you operate. They like the cut of your jib. It's easier for you to get them to come back and spend more. And it's cheaper for you to do that than to go out and actually try to get new people who don't know anything about you.

Oscar Calderon: One hundred percent...I love it. So let's get into it. How do you break it down? What is your process?

Tega Diegbe: It's Dean Jackson's nine word email. I'm sure you've heard of that. Obviously, you're going to need an email list for this. I think people you've had on have talked about building an email list. So you need to have an email list and this is so simple. It is really unbelievable. All you need to do is send an email that says "Are you still interested in ____?" The local businesses I work for are mostly med spas and aesthetic clinics. So they're the ones that do chemical face peels and Botox. As an example, back in October of last year, we started running ads for them that were very, very successful. We ended up generating 200 leads. The leads consist of name and email address. So somebody sees an offer they are interested in on Facebook and they click on it to enter their name and email address.

Of the 200 leads, only 50 of them had actually gone in to claim the advertised offer. Normally, business owners would disregard the other 150 and carry on to try and get new customers. So because I like testing stuff, I said to this client "How about we send this type of email?" The goal of this email will be to get the other 150 leads from October to come in and claim the offer. All we did was send an email with "(First name), are you still interested?" as the subject. The body of the email was "Hi, (first name), you filled in our form on the 12th of October and you were interested in Botox treatments." As an example, we had an offer of 4 units for $25 per unit. I don't know much about aesthetics, but this was really, really cheap. When we sent that, we had a whole bunch of replies and at last check had over 60 replies from people that had given us their name and email address saying, "Yes, I am still interested." Then I had the business follow up with those people manually to get them into the store to actually claim the offer, which puts some money in their pocket. Yes, we spent money to build that list in the first instance, but because we had the list and we could communicate with them, anything that came in was a bonus as far as money made.

Oscar Calderon: That's incredible. And yeah, if you sent to the remaining 150 people that were interested and you got 60 replies, that's almost 30 percent.

Tega Diegbe: Yes, it's about that. The way I work with this business is front end focused. I structured the deal in a way that was front end focused because I wanted to be judged on the results of the front end. Because things were going well, that gave me leeway with the business owner to say, "I think we should try XYZ" and have them be receptive because I've already done something that's worked for them. So if I come back to them with another idea, they're far more likely to try it out and give it a good go rather than just saying, "Oh no, we haven't got the budget for that."

Oscar Calderon: Right. And in terms of the actual leads, they are warm. They are interested. So it's an asset. Once the business owner has that list, it can be used over and over again.

Tega Diegbe: I would like to add to that, though. It's best to follow basic email markets and practices, right? So just because you have the list, doesn't mean you ignore the list until you have something to sell. That's a very quick way to annoy people. This client actually sends out a weekly newsletter of new treatments, tips, and tricks and how to choose the products to buy off the shelf. So they were trying to create a community, but not really one that they could control. They were just giving out content. They had the idea, but hadn't really tried the nine word email. Having been an internet marketer for awhile, it kind of made sense to me as I looked at how much money was being spent on the front end, saw how many people were taking the offer and then saw everybody else who was left, to try and be creative in getting those people to speak up. The goal is to get them to say "Yes, I am still interested" or "Please leave me alone."
Because at the end of the day, it's better to know that they don't want you contacting them and you can remove them from the list instead of continuing to send emails that they are not going to read.

Oscar Calderon: One hundred percent. Life happens. Maybe when they first showed interest, they got distracted. But they are still interested. So you have to follow up.

Tega Diegbe: Yeah, it's basically email retargeting. You have the email list and you just put the offer in front of them again. Retargeting is good on Facebook because our attention spans are so short these days that we may be doing something and then get a notification from a WhatsApp message coming through. We go to click that and get

lost in conversation. And then we forget what we were doing before. So that's why retargeting ads work. This is just a way
of being a little bit more direct without spending any more money by hitting the people that you already have in your database.

Oscar Calderon: Yeah, man. And what I love about this is that you don't have to over complicate things. You don't have to learn about email marketing. It's just literally, "Are you still interested?"

Tega Diegbe: I got this idea from a guy I work with. We have a pretty big email list of entrepreneurs. It is people that mostly work online or want to work online and the email list is engaged, but it's also quite old. And what you tend to find with an old list is your open rate steadily drops, no matter how good of an email you're writing and no matter how engaging it is.
But if someone signs up to your email list and they get distracted, or maybe something happens in life and you send them an email saying, "Are you still interested?", nine out of ten times you're going to get a response. Like I said, it was championed by Dean Jackson. I think he has a course on it. Because I'm on his email list, I got it. He explained the magic of the nine word email. We tried it with the online business and saw how well it worked and thought, why not try it with the local businesses to see if it can work for them as well? It was quite successful, I would say.
Oscar Calderon: That was great. I love it. If people want to know more about you and what you do, where can they find you?

Tega Diegbe: If you want to know more about what I talked about with the nine word email, I can't take credit for it. You have to Google search for Dean Jackson. I think he's on Facebook as well. He runs a podcast called "More Cheese, Less Whiskers" and that's an easy way to find him. If you want to know more about what I'm doing, the easiest way for people to find me right now is on Facebook. I have a website being worked on, but it is not live yet.

Oscar Calderon: Awesome. All right. Take care. Thank you so much for your time. I appreciate it. We'll talk to you soon.

Tega Diegbe: Thank you very much for having me and I hope people get use out of this and actually implement it.

Tega Diegbe

I'm Tega and I help "time stuck" business owners & entrepreneurs go from "Chief Everything Officer" in their business to CEO of their business by building teams, systematising their workflow and leveraging delegation.

EMAIL: tega@tegadiegbe.com

Earl Flormata

Conversation with Earl Flormata

Oscar Calderon: Hey everybody. This is Oscar Calderon and I'm here with Earl Flormata. He is an SEO expert and all around marketing beast. So Earl, how's it going? Thank you for being here.

Earl Flormata: Good. Thanks for having me.

Oscar Calderon: All right. So let's dig in right away. Earl, why don't you tell us who you are, what you do and why we should listen to you?

Earl Flormata: People call me the evil marketing genius because I come up with cockamamie ideas to do marketing online and offline and everywhere else. I've done about 70 million bucks online and offline. So I guess I'm good at it. That's what I do. A hired gun... people hire me to sell stuff.

Oscar Calderon: So let's get into the one thing that we're going to talk about today. What is it?

Earl Flormata: The one thing we're going to talk about today is SEO and how to rank for stuff online.

Oscar Calderon: Great. And why is that important for local business owners in the game?

Earl Flormata: It's important for local business owners because it's how people find everything, right? You know you've made it in the world when you become a verb. So everyone says I'm going to go "Google" something. I'm going to go "Photoshop" something. It becomes a verb. So now that Google has become a verb, I'm going to go Google this. I'm going to Google that. It's literally the first thing that everybody does before they go look for something. I don't care if you are a local restaurant or a local service provider, the first thing people will do to find you is Google you. That is the first place they look to find something.

Oscar Calderon: So for anyone that wants to appear on Google, what are the steps to get there? What are the tricks of the trade?

Earl Flormata: Well, it depends on what you're trying to rank for. So you could rank for your website, your Google business list, or you could rank for your YouTube channel. It depends on what you want people to find. So the first thing is to define how you want to be found. If you're a local brick and mortar store, it kind of makes sense for your Google map listing to show up so people can visit you. If you're an eCommerce store, then you want your best selling products to show up. If you are a service provider, then maybe you want a video or testimonial. So it is defining what you want your first impression to be. Because you have some sort of control over that, you can decide how people will get the first impression. Do you want a video? Do you want audio? Do you want a website? If you're a brick and mortar store, it helps to answer the questions that most of your customers are asking. If your customer service line is always, "Hey, what time do you guys close?", then the hours of operation and the address might be the most effective thing to put on there. So it's whatever your customers ask for the most. You want to make it easy for them to find. That is the first thing you have to do. Once you've got that, then it's time to start optimizing Google for those pieces. The more you put out there, the easier it is for Google to find you. Though this sounds basic, people screw this part up all the time. Don't forget name, address and phone number. There is an acronym for this...NAP. It is all in the little details. For example, how do you spell the word "drive" in your street address? Is it spelled out? Is it all in caps? Does it have one capital letter "D"? Is it just "Dr."? All of those are different addresses to different machines. So you have to be consistent everywhere you go. So those are the basics.

Oscar Calderon: Awesome. So the purpose of all this is to get more exposure, more visibility and transfer those eyeballs because nowadays everyone is looking on Google to find their local businesses. So you better have the fundamentals in place to be seen right away.

Earl Flormata: Yeah. And people don't realize that there's actually three different sets of Google. There is Google desktop, Google on your phone and Google Local, which is on the map. They each will give you different results. So they are all completely different beasts that should be tracked separately.

Oscar Calderon: So you would advise someone to hit those three points separately?

Earl Flormata: Yeah. You have to come up with separate content, separate campaigns, and separate stuff for that sort of thing. If you're on the desktop, that's for heavy lifting. If you want a lot of content or a big, scary article that is 10,000 words long, go for it. But if you want to find a map or you want to optimize for a phone, it'd better be small to fit on the screen nicely or nobody will read the giant string of text. People consume differently based on what device they are on. Nobody on their phone wants to read a wall of text.

Oscar Calderon: One hundred percent. For brick and mortar business owners, Google Maps or Google My Business are the most important things you could optimize to get more business, right?

Earl Flormata: Oh, definitely. Yeah. The way to do that is actually pretty straightforward. At least cover the basics. Because 90% of people don't cover the basics. When you log into Google My Business, fill in every empty field. That's it. Just fill in every empty field. Do you take Visa or MasterCard? All of that stuff is important because the more you provide, the more the client has access to you. Then just be sure that you're pointed in the right direction. We were doing an SEO for a car dealership and they put their address in, but the camera was pointed the wrong way. And instead of pointing at the dealership, it was pointing at an empty field with a cow standing in it. So when people went to look it up, it was really confusing. You went there looking for a dealership but got a cow instead. Turn the camera around, and look...a big, beautiful dealership. We actually have a "wall of shame" that we put this example on.

Oscar Calderon: Some people don't realize that you can claim the listing for free on Google My Business. If you are the business owner, you can claim the listing and enter all of your information. If you don't, chances are that Yelp or other apps will create it for you. You don't want that, right?

Earl Flormata: They'll make it for you and put whatever information they want. You want to have control over your first impression, which is really important. So definitely claim your business page and try to claim as many online sources of the name for your business as possible. There's a really awesome website called namechk.com. If you type in the name of your business, it will actually show you all the things that are open and all the things that are already taken. So it's really useful.

Oscar Calderon: That's a golden nugget right there. I didn't even know about it. And the one thing I want to make clear is that all of this is free. This SEO and claiming your Google My Business is free. You don't have to spend money on this.

Earl Flormata: You don't have to spend money on the basics. Every time I try to explain SEO to somebody I use this joke analogy. There's two guys running away from a bear. And the one guy stops to tie his shoe.Then the other guy freaks out and says, "Why are you tying your shoe? We have to outrun the bear!" The guy says, "I don't have to outrun the bear. I just have to outrun you." That's literally what SEO is. It's how many boxes can you tick ahead of your competitors? How many more things are you doing than them that put you at the top of the list? For example, if you are a restaurant, do you have your menu on your website? Is your menu also on your Google My Business? Is it easily accessible? Is it up to date? Are the prices up to date? All the little things add up. What time are you open on Sundays? All these little, tiny pieces make a big difference. There was a group we worked with about 8 years ago and their literal name was "Dentist on *street name*". I won't name the street, but you would think if you just typed it in you would find them since that was their name. But they ended up doing such a bad job on the basics that you couldn't even find them with their name and street. And every dental client is worth so much money! We advised them to take pictures of the inside of the space and add them to their Google My Business. They have been number one ever since. Again, it is so important to just cover the basics. If you still need more, my company is ready to help and build all of that for you.

Oscar Calderon: Earl, we're at nine minutes and 22 seconds. That was beautiful. Thank you so much. If someone wants more information or wants you to do it for them because they don't have the time or capabilities, where can they find you?

Earl Flormata: My website is mindofamarketer.net, mind of a marketer.net. We'll take care of you.

Oscar Calderon: Thank you. Alright, Earl. Thank you so much. That was great. I appreciate it.

Earl Flormata: No worries.

Oscar Calderon: I'll talk to you soon.

Earl Flormata: Alright. Cheers.

EARL FLORMATA

Mind of a Marketer

Earl Flormata is known as one of the most sought after digital marketing and sales consultants in the Vancouver Marketing arena. He is famous for ranking business and people on Google and has sold over 70 million dollars worth of products and services both on and offline.

Capable of everything from managerial status to running the entire marketing gauntlet himself, Earl can move mountains in any marketing role. Everything from content marketing, authority site building, presentation design and creation, script writing, video creation, marketing and process automation, voiceover work or pitching from a stage to deliver your message - he's a one man Marketing army.

With more than 16 years of sales, marketing and technical experience to bring to the table, the ROI Earl brings is multifaceted. While freelancing, Earl oversees the corporate marketing direction and strategy for multiple companies, including sales, support, consulting, marketing, and alliances and channels. He focuses on strategy, leadership, innovation, creativity, technology and customers.

An educator and public speaker, Earl is a strong evangelist for anything that has great value for people and can help them with their business.

WEBSITE: www.mindofamarketer.net

EMAIL: earl@mindofamarketer.net

Brennan Hopkins

Conversation with Brennan Hopkins

Oscar Calderon: Hey, everybody. I'm Oscar Calderon and being joined by Brennan Hopkins. How are you doing, brother?

Brennan Hopkins: Hello. Thanks so much for chatting with me. I'm doing fantastic. And I appreciate you speaking to me at your time. I'm down in Australia so it's a bit later than your side of the world.

Oscar Calderon: We made it happen. Awesome. So let's dig in. We have 10 minutes so let's start with who you are, what you do, and why we should listen to you?

Brennan Hopkins: Yeah, certainly. I am a direct response copywriter and email marketer, and I've done a ton of work in the email marketing space over the past few years. I work a lot with smaller online businesses to help them make more sales and I've generated multiple millions of sales just through email for my clients. Most notably, one of my clients had a six figure month just through email alone. And so I've been able to get an inside look at a lot of the patterns and behaviors of people and how they respond to email. That's what I'm hoping to be able to share a little bit about today.

Oscar Calderon: I love it, man. Awesome. So with that said, what is the one thing that we're going to talk about right now?

Brennan Hopkins: Boom...right there...emails. But specifically, there's quite a bit that goes into email marketing. So I'm going to focus a bit more on the automated side of things today. I know that is a spot that a lot of business owners often overlook or don't have quite built out as much as they need to and it can be a huge revenue generator for them.

Oscar Calderon: Awesome. So that's the "why", right? Why we should listen to you? Because of all the hidden revenue in this method.

Brennan Hopkins: Well, technically you're building better rapport with your customer base as well. So it kind of goes hand in hand, but yeah...more money.

Oscar Calderon: Alright. So, how do we break it down? What's the process? How do we do it?

Brennan Hopkins: So, there are these platforms called email service providers and they allow store owners and entrepreneurs to build out this really cool mechanical series of emails. Basically, a person goes in and preloads different emails that go out to people on the email list based off of a certain action that they've taken. We've all seen this happen with Amazon. I'm assuming pretty much everyone has shopped with Amazon before. And we get scary accurate emails in our inbox within moments or hours of taking action. That is the principle here.

So the thing I wanted to focus on specifically is called a "welcome series". It is a three to five email series that you would preload for anyone that subscribes to you. It is basically a "who we are" welcome and it is a way to build rapport and capitalize on initial interest. Whenever someone reaches out to you or engages with you, that's a really special opportunity because people are theoretically showing the most interest that they ever will in that moment. And you have a very tiny window to capture their attention or hope that maybe they'll come back one day. So we're basically trying to capitalize on that opportunity to connect, to build rapport and even to incentivize them to stick around and stay connected with your brand.

In a more tangible brick and mortar situation, you would first need to capture someone's email. So a great way you can do that is by some sort of incentive, discount, bonus or special that you give them. For me personally, I see a lot of value in ecommerce stores that offer anywhere from 5-20% off a first time customer's purchase. I would recommend trying to add something of equal value in a tangible brick and mortar so that people want to give you their email because we are looking at the long term. When you get someone on your email list, you're not in it for just the initial sale. You are basically giving yourself the opportunity for two, three, four, or five times the revenue that you're going to get from that customer throughout their experience.

From there, you want to build out a specialized series that automatically goes out to every single person who gave you their email address. Depending on what the sign up is, you may want to include whatever discount or bonus that you promised in the first email, but essentially you are taking advantage of this to indoctrinate the new subscriber about your brand. This is first date worthy stuff. You are blowing the doors open with why you are awesome and why they should want to hang out with you. A lot of times it can sound very braggy and I'm not saying that you should be bragging intentionally, but I'm saying you have a very small window to impress them. Imagine you just met the person of your dreams and you had 30 seconds to impress them. You wouldn't be like "Oh, I made a really good French toast for breakfast." You would be like "I DID THIS..." and that is the goal of the welcome series. You are trying to capture them. But it does go a bit further than just "about me." We're trying to identify the needs of the customer, how we can solve their problem, and simultaneously tie in how awesome we are. But the end result should really be solving their problem. A kind person will certainly hear us out, but most people just care about themselves. So the most effective and persuasive message is one that will resonate on a needs level with the other person. So they realize that not only are we really good, but we are really good for THEIR benefit.

There are lots of different ways to continue to build rapport including customer reviews, stories behind the brands, and unique aspects of your specific offer or product. I would highly recommend any brand to spend some time thinking about what their unique selling proposition is and what makes them a little different. You want to hammer that as well in your email series. And finally, I recommend always including the opportunity to take an action or make a sale. There are some cases where you don't want to ask for the sale, but you pretty much should always be asking people to take some sort of action whether it is checking out your Facebook page, responding to your email, or even checking out some of your products. If you don't, you are basically communicating that you don't think your product is actually worth their time. So why would you show up in their inbox and then not actually believe in your service or product enough to think that they might need it.

Oscar Calderon: If they got into your welcome sequence, they already either bought something from you or they got something for free. So they like you, right? So you might as well sell them more, right?

Brennan Hopkins: Exactly. One hundred percent. The thing is, there are always outliers. We can't build our whole mechanism worried about these few because they are inevitable. So we're trying to maximize the most interested. I've seen this play out in $20,000 to $50,000 that my clients have generated in a month with this type of email series. So even a small brick and mortar store, depending on the amount of subscribers they have, will be looking at thousands of dollars added to their monthly revenue. And it would basically be on autopilot. When it comes to email, we talk about these big companies and stores with huge numbers and they seem so massive that we are like, "that could never happen." But a lot of us are just normal people and that $2,000 extra a month is a big deal. That's a salary, that's bills. Email is so simple to set up and it will return on dividends over and over again forever, theoretically.

Oscar Calderon: Yeah. I love it. One hundred percent. And the best part of all of this is that you could write the emails ahead of time, just throw them in whatever email provider you're working with, and then it does the work for you.

Brennan Hopkins: Yeah, exactly. It is literally that. Microwaving food is harder than this. It's just like waking up to a butler by your bed, handing you X amount of dollars every day, essentially.

Oscar Calderon: Yeah. Or having a salesman, working for you without eating, without getting paid...just working for you 24-7.

Brennan Hopkins: Fantastic. Yeah. That's an awesome example as well.

Oscar Calderon: Brennan, we did 10 minutes and five seconds. Pure fire. I love it, man. If anyone wants more information about email marketing or wants to know more about you and what you do, where can they find you? Where can they go?

Brennan Hopkins: I have my own website, which is brennanwhopkins.com. I'm on Facebook and LinkedIn as well. I try to allocate a bit of time to connect with people each week. So if you want to shoot me a message, I check my message requests. If I have the opportunity, I would be happy to connect with you.

Oscar Calderon: Awesome, brother. Thank you so much for doing this. I’ve got a lot of notes. Talk to you soon.

Brennan Hopkins: All right. Sounds good, man. Have a good one.

Brennan Hopkins

Brennan is a direct response copywriter and email marketing strategist.

His words, strategies, and consulting have generated millions in sales for clients. Brennan's work has also been praised by one of the most successful copywriters of all time, the creator of the Video Sales Letter.

Of course, marketing is just part of Brennan's life. He's also an avid traveler, pizza snob, and dreams of the day when he has a French Bulldog of his very own.

If ANY of the information above sounds like your idea of a good time... odds are you and Brennan could be good friends. Shoot him a message at brennanwhopkins@gmail.com.

WEBSITE: www.brennanwhopkins.com

EMAIL: brennanwhopkins@gmail.com

Keita Hopkinson

How Small Twists In Your Marketing Stories Make For Bigger Sales.

...and the <u>TROJAN HORSE</u> principle for earning prepaid profits.

--by Keita Hopkinson

These musings are for folks with an irrational love of the things they sell...

& who would do it for free--were money not an issue.

*Folks in the <u>arts</u>, or <u>athletics</u>. But certainly **not** limited to them.*

If you, *(like me),* count yourself among these rag-tag tribes--and were offered to be shown a new twist to an ancient principle which can cause you to be…

- ❑ Paid bundles in advance
- ❑ Sped simply to the results for which you yearn
- ❑ Helped to trod a path less cluttered by "grind", fuss, or frustration

Would you be willing to bend an ear to that offer?

Stories are woven through the fabric of our DNA.

In marketing--stories *appropriate to the customer's situation* are the best leverage for inspiring the results you seek.

You can strengthen the impact of your marketing stories by using...

METAPHORS--aimed at triggering as many senses as possible in your customer.

Metaphors that appeal to sight, smell, sound, touch, etc.--give grit, and grab--like the treads of a running shoe give you traction.

Customers are frantic now...

They appreciate clarity.

A clear message

if it's the right message

to the right customer

at the right time

in the right tone

Helps you to better serve your customer

--AND gets you paid for your trouble.

Metaphors can bring clarity to stories.

The thing you do when thirsty--which you MUST also do for stories to attract profit to your business.

(HINT: you've gotta do this before you drink!)

If there's no traction to your story, it's much like wanting juice from an orange--yet refusing to squeeze it.

The orange is sitting there, right?

The juice is inside that orange.

But you need to SQUEEZE the thing to get it out.

Similarly, you might have something--*(a product and story)*--which can connect with your customer.

A thing with which your prospect might resonate.

A nugget that might help improve their life and work.

But unless you find a way…

(...especially with all the fret, and frustration, and the noise and the folly--and all of the stuff that's spilling now)...

If you don't find a way

...to drive home to them

...the good you can do *for* them

Then *that* possibility will atrophy from sitting idle.

NOW, while this is a cute and useful tip--it won't pull the biggest levers in the mechanism of your sales.

What follows next can move monster gears in your business.

How The TROJAN HORSE Principle Pays You Upfront--*AND* On The Backend.

The "TROJAN HORSE" principle refers to an 8,500+ year old Greek poem about war--that can be used to build goodwill & good vibes between market competitors, and coinage for all involved.
(There are at least 6 ways that you can PROFIT from this--for FREE!)

QUICK SUMMARY: The TROJAN HORSE Story...

This ancient poem speaks of a huge statue of a horse being delivered to a tribe as a "gift".

Once delivered, the enemies of the tribe emerged from the hollowed-out belly of the beast.

(Sneak attack).

Here's how stories can help you to get PAID to promote your products for free.

The "TROJAN HORSE" principle is a variation on famed marketer Gary Halbert's "Co-Op MAILER" concept...

As a marketer, here's what you might do...

1--Put together a monthly digital newsletter that your customer looks forward to receiving.

2--Get a dozen or so non-competing businesses *for the same customer*--to PAY you to include their advertorials in your newsletter.

(If you're a copywriter--you can write the advertorials too).

3--Fees paid to you by these businesses, cover the cost of the project. *Ideally--aim to profit on the front end.*

4--Add-in your own advertorials--For Free

6 ways you can earn from this...

1--Subscription fees--*(unless it's a free newsletter)*

2--Advertisers pay you to host their promotions

3--They pay you to write their promotions

4--They pay you a monthly continuity fee to keep ads in

5--Sell your own products in the newsletter

6--Sell affiliate products

Six streams of income make it easier for you to make each one of those steps affordable for the people you serve.

You can also get into bartering, referrals, strategic partnerships--each of which helps you to build goodwill now--which will serve you in long-term.

Historic Examples.

Magazines, Comic Books, Pulp Fiction publications, and Newspapers have done this for eons...

- ❑ Cliff-hanger, continuity stories.
- ❑ With Ads tucked in back.
- ❑ Delivered daily, weekly, monthly.

J.Peterman catalogs create fictional backstories for products in their catalog.

This adds personality. Enhances appeal. Helps generate sales.

The simple mechanism of alchemy

...which turns a *"boring hunk of tin"* into hundreds of millions in sales each year!

(TIP: Disney & Marvel use it. Why not you?)

Here's something I picked up from copywriter/marketer guru-figure, Colin Theiot...

In the 1980s, toy manufacturers had action figures to sell.

They hired writers & animators to create Saturday Morning Cartoons, featuring their toys as characters.

This was essentially, ½ hour long commercials--marketed to children.

Children harassed their parents--who bought the toys.

Wait, wot?? Stories made a hunk of tin --appealing enough to cause a sale.

Stories & metaphors are tools of alchemy. They move us _*from*_ *where we are--*_*to*_ *where we wish to be.*

Worth a shot.

If there are things you cherish in life that depend on sales you make--*(especially when it comes to your preferred use of your **time**)*--these principles can work in your favour.

The concepts are sound--proven by eons of toil.

Not to be an alarmist--*(ok, maybe just slightly)*--think **not** just of what might happen if these ideas were to work for you.

But percolate also on *what you might lose* if you choose to ignore them.

BIO:

Keita Hopkinson is…

a Painter

Direct Response Marketer

Copywriter

Swing concert Promoter /Impresario.

...with a background in athletics.

He's intrigued with thought launching simple kitchen-table projects to help artists he knows;

painters/illustrators/authors, swing musicians
athletes & practitioners in health/fitness spaces

--to get paid for doing what they love.

THEN, he uses those projects as a platform for building affiliate opportunities ***for businesses that serve those markets as well.***

Hopkinson has worked with select members of Grammy winning jazz bands.

He's looking into the possibility of working with UFC fighters

Olympic track athletes

...and artists who've created classic art for galleries **&** for franchises like Star Wars, Marvel, MTG, and fiction book publishing.

EMAIL: khopkinson@yahoo.com

Ryan Hunter

Conversation with Ryan Hunter

Oscar Calderon: Hey, everybody. I'm Oscar and I'm joined by the "Hunter". Ryan Hunter is a copywriting extraordinaire, but I'm going to let you introduce yourself. What's up, Ryan. How's it going?

Ryan Hunter: Hey, everybody. Thank you so much for interviewing me and bringing me on. This is going to be great. My name is Ryan Hunter and I'm what's known as a profit leverage consultant. I essentially go in and I find assets. I help people find those gold mines in their business and then turn them into actual gold.

Oscar Calderon: Awesome. Ryan, what is the one thing that we're going to learn today?

Ryan Hunter: I'll give you two quick reasons why you should listen to me. The first company I ever worked with was a solar company and I changed up their whole online marketing and their website. And the first year I was there, they did half a million with their website. The next year, after I redesigned it and changed some things around, they did 1.5 million. So they added a million dollars in revenue just from their website. Secondly, I worked with a client and helped him make over a hundred thousand dollars from one single Facebook post, just by finding the right way of positioning an idea. So those are some of the things that I've done and why I'm not just a "yahoo" off the street.

Oscar Calderon: Wow. Might have to get you a second interview to talk about that one post idea. Tell us what we are going to talk about today.

Ryan Hunter: We're going to talk about strategic partnerships, joint ventures and utilizing other businesses' assets so that you can get more customers and sales in a very easy way that you may not have thought about before.

Oscar Calderon: I love it. Why is that important to local brick and mortar business owners?

Ryan Hunter: Everybody needs sales and revenue and you need customers for that. A lot of people are not aware of all the ways that you can generate new customers. You know when you are in a race and you can draft behind somebody and you can go a little bit faster because you're not against all that air resistance? It's kind of similar. You can leverage somebody else's efforts and harvest a bunch of customers very quickly and affordably, sometimes even completely free. It brings a flood of new customers into your business and a few phone calls is all it could really take.

Oscar Calderon: That's awesome. I cannot wait and I'm sure everyone can't wait. So let's dive in. How do you do it? How do you create those strategic partnerships and joint ventures successfully?

Ryan Hunter: So the first thing is, and this might sound a little ruthless, but a lot of businesses are going to go out of business and those businesses have assets. So look at the competitors in your area and see if there are people closing their doors. You can then go and buy their customer list that they have spent years and probably tens of thousands of dollars building. These are targeted lists of ideal prospects. You can go in and buy that from them as a business asset for pennies on the dollar. And then you have a list that you can do prospecting from. You can send mail to their past customers and invite them to work with you. And those people are perfectly suited to become your next customers. So that's one way.

The next one is striking a deal. First you must understand the term "indirect competitor". It means people that serve the same type of a customer as you, but you're not directly competing. So, what's a good example?

Oscar Calderon: Let's go with gyms.

Ryan Hunter: So let's say you are the owner of a gym trying to get members back after the quarantine. People who come to the gym are people that take care of themselves, care about their appearance, and value being healthy. So you find another business that may have a similar clientele. A hair salon, for example. You can go to the hair salon and say "Hey, do you mind if I send a piece of mail to everyone on your customer list inviting them to a free trial at my gym? Would that be cool?" And they say "Sure, that sounds good!" Maybe that hair salon has had a thousand customers over the past 10 years, and then you could just send an email or an actual letter to those thousand people. And now you've got people coming into your gym and you didn't have to put up a bus sign, a newspaper ad or some other advertisement where everybody sees it. You're just sending it to people that care about their looks and their health. Just think about all the businesses that serve similar clientele and then go strike up a deal with them where you're leveraging their asset, their customer list or their email list in order to promote your business.

Oscar Calderon: Yeah. And these are people that are buyers or clients that pay money. So they're targeted, right? If you do your due diligence and you find out where your customers are and what non-competing businesses they are hanging out in, you can strike up a deal. If you have a gym and a nutritionist, for example, there is a correlation there and you can use the nutritionist clients to strike up that deal. And then you have these laser targeted prospects coming towards you.

Ryan Hunter: And you can change how you structure the deal. You know, maybe what you do is say "Hey, you're a nutritionist. I'm a jiu jitsu gym. Can I promote you? I will send an email or a letter to all my customers and promote your services. And then you do the same." Now you're cross pollinating and you're helping each other. And you can nail that down in one phone call. And if it's an email, there's no cost. If it's direct mail, the costs are going to be negligible. So there are many, many ways that you can apply this same sort of concept.

Oscar Calderon: That's amazing, man. Strategic partnerships are definitely one of the keys to grow your business in an affordable way and laser target.

Ryan Hunter: And if you're a nutritionist, for example, and you live in any decent sized town or city, you can drum up deals with every single gym, every single martial arts studio and every single health food store. So now instead of having just one source, you could have 20, 30, 40 sources of new customers. Maybe they send just one per month each, but now you've got this constant flood of people. And what's great is you are now antifragile. If you've got a three legged stool and you knock one of those legs out, the whole stool falls. When you have all these different streams of new clientele from your partners, now you've got a 20 legged stool. And even if one of those stops, you're still safe. You're still sturdy. So you build a lot of redundancy and safety in your business that way.

Oscar Calderon: Yeah, exactly. And let's say you're a gym owner and you strike a deal with a nutritionist. And that pitch that you gave them worked. So now you have a working pitch. So you can use that pitch to keep getting more.

Ryan Hunter: Yes. This is outside of the scope, but if that works, you could even get into a different business and sell the strategy to other people in other states. You could say, "Hey, do you want to create a stream of new clients?" So that pitch is an asset that you can reuse or that you can sell to other people in different places.

Oscar Calderon: I love it, brother. I'm all about extracting hidden assets that you have in your business that you just weren't aware of. It's the most economic part of it too, because you're not wasting any money or spending money in ads or anything. Ryan, if the people reading or watching this are interested in finding out more about strategic partnerships and joint ventures, where can they find you?

Ryan Hunter: So it's a very short web address and that will take you to my domain, my place. My last name is Hunter. So the web address is hntr.to. So just go to hntr.to and that will bring you to my place. And then we can go from there.

Oscar Calderon: Awesome, brother. This was fire, man. Thank you so much for it. We'll talk to you soon.

Ryan Hunter: Alright, thank you.

Ryan Hunter

Ryan Hunter is a long-form direct-response copywriter and consultant. He works with some of the largest brands in the health space. One of his unique approaches to copy is his skill with storytelling. Ryan is a master of using story to overcome the reader's objections without them realizing it.

His direct response consultancy, Arch Conversions LLC, helps brands scale on cold traffic by optimizing Conversions and Average Order Value.

He is also the co-founder of Availant Health, a rapidly growing holistic supplement company.

An interesting tidbit about Ryan is that he enjoys working in the fields of Artificial Intelligence and Software Development for fun. In fact, after teaching himself to code at the age of 13, Ryan went on to develop software that would be used in the school system, the music industry and the solar industry.

Outside of business, Ryan's life calling is centered around youth mentorship. His passion is to create resources to support boys raised without strong father figures.

Now, Ryan mentors multiple men ranging from ages 16 to 38 on the subjects of both business and life.

As of July 2020, it costs $19,200 to hire Ryan for an in-person consulting day, $10,000 upfront plus royalties if you want him to write a sales letter.

However, Ryan is always open to helping those who are willing to ask. So don't be shy to reach out.

WEBSITE: ryanhunter.io

EMAIL: ryan@ryanhunter.io

Pedro Meneses

Conversation with Pedro Meneses

Oscar Calderon: I am Oscar Calderon. I'm being joined by Pedro Meneses. How's it going, Pedro?

Pedro Meneses: How's it going, guys? Thank you for having me here. It's going great. What about you?

Oscar Calderon: I'm good. I'm excited to find out what we are going to talk about today. So why don't we just dig in right away? Please tell us who you are, what you do and why we should listen to you?

Pedro Meneses: Absolutely, man. My name is Pedro Meneses and I am the owner and founder of the Marketing Brewing Company. We actually help breweries to generate more customers and sales and sell more beer through online and social media marketing. We build what is called a digital taproom, which is basically a system to help convert all those followers, likes and comments into real paying customers. We achieve this through selling online or driving more fluid traffic into your brewery, obviously when this pandemic is over..

Oscar Calderon: Awesome. So with that said, what is the one thing we're going to talk about today?

Pedro Meneses: First of all, the reason why this is important for breweries to understand is because these times have taught us how crucial it is to have an online presence. It is the only way we can promote any business and keep selling our products or services. Right? I think that's why it's important to not only focus on a short term strategy, but also on a long term one where you can leverage the power of social media to keep generating more sales and customers. Before this virus happened, there were already 74% of craft beer drinkers searching and buying beer online. I'm sure that percentage will go even higher in the next couple of months. The challenge is that no one has taken the time to build and set up a system that can take each potential customer from being a like or a follower, to somebody walking into your brewery two or three times a week or buying online. Social media marketing is the fastest and most cost effective way to generate more sales, but it goes beyond making posts and getting followers. One thing that I always say to my current clients is that you cannot deposit likes, comments and followers. You need to know who your target audience is. You have to communicate effectively and create a customer journey that will drive more people into your brewery or online taproom. So that's basically the system that we have built for breweries in order for them to increase beer sales and scale their breweries as well.

Like I mentioned before, we create what we call a digital taproom that I will talk about in a minute. This system helps separate your target audience from the rest and converts them to repeat customers. To everyone listening or reading this right now... you are not the only ones advertising out there. There are plenty of other businesses in the craft beer industry trying to get more people to sell their beer to. So when you don't have a system that can help separate that target audience, it’s going to be hard for them to remember you. This is basically what the digital taproom does. We do this through organic and paid advertising on social media and we use sales funnels, automation, emails and text campaigns to generate more subscribers and build your database. The ultimate goal is to make more sales. We do this through organic marketing and Facebook ads. Then, we drive all of that traffic to landing pages. This is important because we need to have a specific journey to create new customers. These landing pages can be for new events, new releases and brewery updates on a weekly or monthly basis. And the goal is to drive more traffic to your online ordering due to the circumstances of the pandemic right now. But make sure that every single person that is clicking on these landing pages is being called to take action so they can order beer online and come pick it up. If you are available to deliver, obviously deliver your beer. Eventually, when we go back to normal after the pandemic, the goal will be to get more butts in seats at your actual taproom. The whole point of this is to create and help you build your database or subscriber list. I will get to this in a second and why it is important. For example, you can put QR codes everywhere in your taproom and invite your customers to subscribe to your list so they can be informed about upcoming events. It is easy to get them to do this, especially if you say "If you scan the code and join right now, you get 10% off your tap today." Who is going to say "no" to that? It will not only help you get more subscribers on your list, but it will help increase sales because you are giving your customers something of value...something they will appreciate from you as a business. After you have this subscriber list created, you can target them later through email, retargeting ads and text messaging to keep them in this cycle and buying your beer over and over again. This will increase your revenue as a business.

Oscar Calderon: One hundred percent. The best part is, you are building an asset with this list and you can use it again and again.

Pedro Meneses: Yeah, absolutely. And this system can be suited to your specific needs. How many events do you have? Have you partnered with food trucks? Do you have other small businesses that you partner with? For example, here in Dallas, there are breweries that do yoga events on Saturdays and they partner with these yoga studios and help each other out. So we can adapt it all to your needs. We are realizing now, more than ever, that no matter what industry you are in, you can still leverage social media and the internet to make sales. So after the pandemic is over, if you combine your social media strategies and keep driving physical traffic into your brewery, your numbers are just going to go through the roof. And that's the goal of the digital taproom.

Oscar Calderon: Wow. I love it, man. Awesome. Pedro, thank you for this. If people want to find out more information about the digital taproom and what you do, where can they find you?

Pedro Meneses: They can find me on Facebook or Instagram. You'll find me on Facebook under my name...Pedro Meneses. My profile is open to the public and is basically my business card. On Instagram, you can find me at Marketing Brewing Co. You can visit the website marketingbrewingco.com, fill out the form and we can get on a free consultation call. I also have a Facebook group for craft beer professionals called the Brewing Business Network. We provide tools and resources for all different aspects of business including loans and finances, specifically for craft beer professionals. You can also listen to my podcast that is called the "Brewing Business Show." You can find it on Spotify or Anchor FM, and soon it's going to be available on iTunes. I bring in different guests, not only from the craft beer industry, but from other industries to share their experience or knowledge. You can learn what they have done in their lives through their entrepreneur journeys and apply it to your business as a brewery.

Oscar Calderon: That's great, man. Awesome. Thank you so much for doing this. Thank you for your time. I appreciate it. Talk to you soon, Pedro.

Pedro Meneses: Thanks to you, man. I really appreciate you having me here and giving me the space to share with your audience. I'm grateful for it. Thank you so much.

Pedro Meneses

A natural-born leader, driven by passion and always committed to delivering excellence to everyone he helps and surrounds himself with.

Pedro was born and raised in Guatemala City. From a very young age, he always showed signs of independence, leadership, and great ambition.

During his first years as an adult, Pedro always believed that life was more than just getting a degree, a 9-5 job, a family, and following orders until the day he dies.

Thirsty for answers to his deepest desires and goals, when Pedro turned 25, he decided to leave his country, his family, and everything that was known to him to pursue a greater dream, purpose, and his career as an entrepreneur.

Pedro is best known for being someone bold in his actions and for always speaking and leading with the truth. As a respected entrepreneur in his field, Pedro has been a guest and featured on several influential podcasts.

He is also the host of The Brewing Business Show, a podcast dedicated to the craft beer industry and like-minded entrepreneurs.

He is the owner and founder of The Marketing Brewing Company, an industry-leading digital marketing provider and coaching firm serving the craft beer industry. He also offers marketing services to other industries along with his beautiful wife, Kayla Meneses, and together they also own a Real Estate business.

He is on a mission to help brewery owners improve their businesses and lives so that they can have a larger impact on their community and families.

"Get It Done….Be Unstoppable!"

WEBSITE: www.marketingbrewingco.com

EMAIL: pedro@marketingbrewingco.com

Ben Stocks

Conversation with Ben Stocks

Oscar Calderon: This is Oscar and I'm here with local business marketer, Ben Stocks. How are you doing, man?

Ben Stocks: Good. Thanks for having me, man.

Oscar Calderon: This is only going to be 10 minutes, so we're going to dive right in. No nonsense. Let's go. So Ben, tell us who you are, what you do and why we should listen to you?

Ben Stocks: My name is Ben Stocks and I help local businesses grow. I mainly work with gyms. I owned one for six years and eventually sold it. I started doing that when I was super young, just figuring out life, trying to make things work and discovering marketing along the way to scale my business up. Then I started reaching out and providing others with ways to do the same for their businesses. So much so, that I sold the gym and went full time into what I am doing now, which is helping local businesses grow.

Oscar Calderon: What are we going to be talking about today? What actionable tactic will you be discussing?

Ben Stocks: I would consider this more of a principle than a tactic. And it's something that you can apply all across the board. Simply stated, it is the idea of zigging when everyone else is zagging. As entrepreneurs, we all want to do that, right? We want to think differently and stand out from the competition, obviously. Now, at the time of this interview, the coronavirus is going on and things are crazy. So now more than ever, I think we need to pivot. I am a big fan of Dan Kennedy and I remember him telling a story back in the day at a seminar. It's an old oral Nightingale story. The gist of it was if you're a young person wanting to be successful and you don't have a mentor, just look around you and see what everyone else is doing. Then do the opposite and you will be 90% of the way there. If we all do what everyone else is doing, we're never going to "speak" to anyone.

Oscar Calderon: If we were to break down your process to do this in chunks, how would we achieve it?

Ben Stocks: Let's take a look at an example related to what we have going on right now with the global
pandemic known as Coronavirus. We have two groups of people, one of which is in conservation mode. They are like "batten down the hatches", don't spend any money, and we are just going to wait this thing out. Essentially, this is the "hoping and waiting" group. It is somewhat wishful thinking, since we really don't know how long this thing is going to last and what the world will look like after.

On the other hand, we have the group saying "I am going to take advantage of this time because all of my competitors are dropping out." I just made a post about this the other day. It's like if you were going into a competition with big prize money on the line and you had been training your whole life for this. You realize as the competition is coming up that the competitors are all dropping out. There is no way you wouldn't show up to the competition because you figure there is no way you can lose. Even if you aren't feeling your best, you are going to win this thing because all of the competition is conserving, running and hiding. Now is the time to push and grab as much market share as possible because you are not all competing for the same slice of the pie. You have got the whole pie right in front of you. In my opinion, now is the time to go out and grab as much market share as humanly possible while competition is low.

Oscar Calderon: What are some steps to take in order to accomplish this?

Ben Stocks: If you don't have the resources, it is what it is. If you were not able to save and build a big chunk of resources that you can now use, maybe you have to batten down the hatches and just ride this wave out. But if you've got the resources, advertising is on sale right now. You can get leads so cheap because there is no competition. Nobody is spending money and everyone is hiding. Many local businesses are thinking "Hey, my doors are closed, so why should I even market?" I believe that is a mistake because there are a lot of ways you can make money and serve people. Again, if you have the resources and are willing to spend a bit to grab market share, now is the time.

Secondly, you should really try to explore new niches that you didn't serve in the past because you thought your competitors already had a strong foothold in them. Try to serve them and build up a ton of goodwill so that when everyone does reopen, they will immediately look past the competitors and straight to you for helping them. Odds are, your competition is not serving them during this time. The biggest danger of being in that first group of people who are just conserving right now is coming back to a world with much smaller lists of people who want to work with them. This is the perfect time to plant those seeds so that when we return to a certain sense of normalcy, those seeds have already been watered and you can reap the benefits. A mentor of mine told me the other day that "winter is the time to buy fields." Your competitors may have been hiding all winter in hibernation. You will have those fields to benefit from if you are a good steward now, going after those fields and grabbing that market share.

Oscar Calderon: Like you said, if you are thinking of using paid ads, they are cheaper than ever. So you might as well.

Ben Stocks: Yes. Everyone is stuck at home now. They are checking their phones and they're bored. They are looking for things to do and people to serve them. We're entrepreneurs, right? We can find creative ways to serve people. And your messaging may not be "Hey, pay me all this money", but talk to their pain. Speak to their pain right now. All that you need to do is find a way to touch pain points and be empathetic towards people and connect that to a product or a service. And that's your job as a business owner right now. Think of those niches and those people who are not being served right now and are not being reached out to. If you're going to do it and your competition is going to sleep through it, I think that you deserve the rewards.

Oscar Calderon: A hundred percent I'm with you. Do you have anything you would like to add?

Ben Stocks: I think that covers it. I would just say, if you have the resources, don't be afraid to be aggressive in your marketing. Advertising is on sale right now. Competition is low. So why not take advantage of that? Why would you wait until everyone else is going to start marketing again to market? And this can be applied across the board. So in a year from now when hopefully this whole thing is over, don't do what everyone else is doing. Why would you play on the same field that everyone is playing on? Why would you go to where all the competition is? It's that blue ocean/red ocean strategy, right? I want to play in a blue ocean. I don't want to go in the red ocean and get beat up. I'd rather go where the competition is low. And so be aggressive with your marketing if you have the resources because now is the time to stake out a bigger share of the market. Build up goodwill in niches that you feel like you weren't able to tap into before because your competition had too strong of a foothold. When this is all turned around, those people will come to you as opposed to your competitors.

Oscar Calderon: If anyone wants more information about how to advertise in the world we live in, how can they get in contact with you?

Ben Stocks: I'm a big fan of just friending me on Facebook. I market on Facebook and Instagram a lot. So I like to communicate with people there. It is just my personal profile. Feel free to send me a friend request or a message and I would be happy to chat.

Oscar Calderon: Awesome. Ben, thank you so much for this. I appreciate it. We'll talk to you soon.

Ben Stocks: Thanks man. I appreciate it.

BEN STOCKS

Ben Stocks Marketing

Ben Stocks has been an entrepreneur since a young age. At 20 years old, he started a gym. Soon after, he realized the power of marketing to grow his gym and fell in love with helping other local business owners grow their businesses. Six years later, Ben sold his gym to focus full time on helping local businesses (particularly gyms) and some online businesses increase their profits beyond levels they originally imagined possible using smart, ethical and POWERFUL marketing strategies.

WEBSITE: www.meetingwithben.com

EMAIL: benstocksmarketing@gmail.com

FACEBOOK: https://www.facebook.com/ben.stocks.7

PHONE: 443-903-4553

Scott Sylvan Bell

Conversation with Scott Sylvan Bell

Oscar Calderon: All right. Here we are with Scott. How's it going man?

Scott Sylvan Bell: Hey, Oscar! It's going well.

Oscar Calderon: Today we are going to talk for about ten minutes about specific things business owners can do to survive and get business done in this crazy time. Why don't you start with letting us know who you are and why we should listen to you?

Scott Sylvan Bell: Absolutely. My name is Scott Sylvan Bell. I'm based out of Sacramento, California. Over the last ten years, I've been working undercover, behind the scenes with companies, helping out salespeople and helping out communications. So whether it's me doing a ride along with a salesperson or sitting side by side in the call center, I help people realize where they can improve. I've worked with companies at a million dollars. I've worked with companies at fifty million dollars. I've worked with Fortune 100 companies. Whether it's communication face to face like this, body language, or conversation...these are all things that I specialize in.

Oscar Calderon: Awesome. So what is the one thing that we're going to learn today in ten minutes?

Scott Sylvan Bell: Absolutely. You have a few seconds, a few minutes to impact the people that you meet with, and that's all you got. I'll just start from the very beginning. This is one of the biggest struggles that I see companies and salespeople face. A company pays for marketing. They pay for a click. They pay for a lead. A phone call comes into the call center at the office. And the people who are answering the phone can't answer the ten most simple, frequently asked questions. They can't get to the point and say, "Hey, here's what's going on", so they constantly have to put people on hold. Somebody will call and they'll say, "Hey, I want help with my problem." And the person in the call center will say, "I don't know if we do that, hold on", and CLICK, puts them on hold. People are patient, but eventually they get to the point where they are like "How do you not know this? I'm calling you. It's what your company does. Why can't you tell me what you do?" If you have an organization, there are ten to fifteen questions that are consistently asked. You should know the answers to those. Every person on the team should be scripted and know how to fix problems and deal with issues.

Oscar Calderon: Right. Because there's a disconnect there. If the salesperson doesn't know, it could lead to a very negative outcome.

Scott Sylvan Bell: When somebody makes a phone call, they're thinking to themselves, how confident can I be as a consumer that everything's going to work out? And if in those first two or three minutes, that somebody looks around and says, this guy can't even answer my questions, it creates a lot of problems for your company. Why would they want to continue the conversation? If you have anyone who has worked for you for any amount of time, you can say, "What are the top three questions you're asked?" Do this with the entire team and create a file. When you train somebody brand new, they don't get to be on the floor until they can answer those ten questions. They don't get to interact with buyers until they know all the facts and information. Then they aren't saying "Please hold while I go look that up", and then jumping back on the line.

Oscar Calderon: How do you create a quality FAQ with the ten most important questions so that there's no disconnect?

Scott Sylvan Bell: Like I mentioned, we would grab a team and we would sit everybody in a room and we would say, "Allright, out of everything that you're asked during the day, what are the ten most frequently asked questions that you get?" The team gets together, they give the information and they may come up with twenty. This is the critical frontline information that people need to know about a company. How could you not have a team trained to handle these questions? This is happening with salespeople too. It isn't just a phone call center issue. This is across the board with organizations. You can do the same thing with HR...what are the ten most frequently asked questions to HR? You can do this with every department inside your organization. It will streamline things a whole lot faster.

Oscar Calderon: As you said, this is very important when it comes to sales because it is the first line, right? This is where people are coming in. So you have to give a great first impression. But it isn't just that. Once they know those ten questions, any local business owner could now shift their messaging, marketing and advertising based on those questions, right?

Scott Sylvan Bell: Sure. They may be marketing to the wrong people. They may have the wrong message like the insight you gathered. Here is the breakdown. You should have ten frequently asked questions, ten "should ask" questions and ten common mistakes that people make. So there's actually 30 things that you need. Let's start with the ten frequently asked questions. What are the ten most frequently asked questions? What should you be asking? And what are the most common mistakes made in the industry?

Oscar Calderon: Now you mentioned "should ask" questions. That's very interesting because in our industry, a lot of people don't dive really deep into "should ask" questions. And they're very important, right?

Scott Sylvan Bell: Yes. And what's weird is people don't think in terms of what they should be asking until they get on the phone with a buyer. And this is why I'm a huge fan of where possible and legal, you record a presentation or a phone call and any question that is asked gets automatically dropped into a document. You have training capital in everything that you do. So you get one of those messages that says "this call is recorded for quality and training purposes". Here's what you are going to do. You're going to take that audio, dump it into something like otter.ai, and put every question that is asked into a PDF so that brand new employees can search the information, memorize it, and be quizzed on it. And the same thing should be happening for "should ask" questions. People say, "What should I be asking?" So if someone said to me right now, "Scott, what should I be asking?", I would say, "You should be asking, how long should this take?" And my answer is "not very long". It should take maybe an hour or two. You get a team together. You ask the questions and you put them into a document. You say, "from here on out, these are the ten things you have to know to work here, to interact, and then we are good to go."

Oscar Calderon: And now they can represent your business the right way, how it should be represented.

Scott Sylvan Bell: Absolutely. And it's amazing how many times companies just can't answer these questions. It doesn't matter how big or small the industry, they just don't have this down. And if you don't have this down, what else do you not have?

Oscar Calderon: You mentioned frequently asked questions, "should ask" questions, and then there's a third category...

Scott Sylvan Bell: Common mistakes people make. This is where reviews come in. People read reviews so they don't make a mistake. If the review says "I like the product. It's amazing. It's fantastic. But it's got a problem with the power cord." Well, I don't want to make that mistake of buying something with a bad power cord. So a review is a reverse "don't make this mistake."

Oscar Calderon: Gotcha. That's gold, man. That's classic. Alright, man. So for the breakdown, you have 30 questions with answers which include frequently asked questions, "should ask" questions and common mistakes. And obviously that's great for salespeople right on the front line, but could also be used in your marketing, advertising, emails and your communication with your clients. It helps you to gather information.

Scott Sylvan Bell: Yes. And the thing is too, once you have ten frequently asked questions, ten "should ask" questions and ten common mistakes, you now have a buyer's guide. Now you don't have to necessarily say it all the time. You have an asset you could deploy and somebody could download that information as a lead generation source. There's a method to the madness.

Oscar Calderon: That's even better. So you could use these documents not only to train your salespeople, but to share with your buyer.

Scott Sylvan Bell: Yes. You're going to share it with your buyer. It's going to show that you're responsible enough. It's going to show them that you're prepared and you've thought through their buying process and it helps build confidence. Like... "You read my mind. How did you know that I was thinking about these questions? How did you know that I was worried about looking dumb in front of someone?" When we make a purchase, we have people in our surroundings that will criticize that decision. They're going to say, "I could have gotten it for less. That's not a good product." And so when you have backup information that says "I already know the answer to the question you are going to ask me. I already know how you're going to criticize me. I already know how to deal with that objection." It's not like you have to worry about what's going on in your own head. You have to worry about all the people around you who are going to criticize what you've done. Now you've got the answer. I already know the answer, so you can't criticize me on this.

Oscar Calderon: Also, it helps because if a buyer is confused, you pretty much lost them. Right? So it streamlines your sales process. That was awesome, Scott.. We literally did nine minutes and 30 seconds. If anyone is interested in finding out more about your process and everything that you do to help business owners, where can they go?

Scott Sylvan Bell: I have my main website where my podcast is. I'm building it out right now. It's howtosell.live. There is contact information. You can call my business line or text me on my business line, which is (808) 364-9906. That is a Hawaii number. I'll do whatever I can to help out and point you in the right direction. If I don't know the answer, I'll tell you that and direct you to someone who does.

Oscar Calderon: Scott, thank you so much for this. It really means a lot. It already helped me come up with ideas for my own business, and I'm sure this is going to help a lot of local business owners. So thank you so much.

Scott Sylvan Bell: And then I have one last resource. If you go to howtosell.live/create, there's a list that you could download of 250 different ways of coming up with content. And there's a cheat sheet for the top ten frequently asked questions, top ten "should ask" questions, and the ten common mistakes that people make.

Oscar Calderon: Beautiful. I'll be checking that out too. Thank you so much, Scott. Thank you for your time. I'll talk to you soon.

Scott Sylvan Bell

Scott Sylvan Bell is a Trainer, Coach and Mentor for Salespeople as well as Business Owners. He holds an MBA in Business and Marketing.

Scott specializes in creative solutions to common problems with communication through written, audio and video content.

With over 2,600 YouTube videos on Sales, Persuasion, Storytelling, Body Language and Decision Making, content creation became a focal point of his creativity.

Scott has created multiple cheat sheets and training guides to help salespeople and companies successfully prepare for interactions with their clients.

For the last decade, Scott has been working behind the scenes with companies and salespeople. These interactions lead to insights that help with better interaction with not just training, but also with clients.

These interactions lead to the framework for his Frequently Asked Questions (FAQ), Should Ask Questions (SAQ) and (CAQ) Commonly Asked Questions guides. These assets are meant to reduce the friction your buyer faces to make a purchase easier.
In turn, these guides and trainings make your sales process quicker for the clients, as well as the office staff. When you add these guides to your marketing plan, you create a competitive advantage. Scott teaches how to use these techniques and technologies to outperform your competition.

It's not uncommon to find Scott working in a Reyn Spooner Button Down Aloha shirt. He says the louder and wilder the print, the better.

When not working on the Mainland, you can find Scott on the Island of Oahu catching up on his suntan, watching Big Wave Surfing or creating content.

You can find more ways to creatively create content at:

https://howtosell.live/create
@scottsbell
#scottbellisawesome

WEBSITE: https://howtosell.live/

EMAIL: scott_sylvan@yahoo.com

Mark Tandan

Conversation with Mark Tandan

Oscar Calderon: Hey, everybody. This is Oscar Calderon being joined today by Mark Tandan. How's it going, Mark?

Mark Tandan: Excellent. Thanks, Oscar. Thanks for having me.

Oscar Calderon: Thank you for being here. These are 10 minute interviews so let's dive right in, please. Mark, tell us who you are, what you do and why we should listen to you?

Mark Tandan: Well, listening to me is always your choice. But I am a copywriter. I've been copywriting full time for the last five years. Prior to that, I spent many years in both retail and hospitality. I did some consulting in Omnichannel, particularly online marketing in their retail outlets. I also helped out with recruitment within college programs in their hospitality fields. So I've got a lot of boots to the ground experience in not just the digital world, but actual brick and mortar stores as well.

Oscar Calderon: Awesome. I love it. So, what is the one thing we are going to talk about today?

Mark Tandan: I'd like to chat briefly about increasing customer value from existing customers. A lot of focus is on how to get new business and how to find new customers. But we all know it's easier and cheaper to keep a customer than to go out and get one. I have some practical tips on how to maximize that relationship.

Oscar Calderon: Awesome. Why is this important for local business owners?

Mark Tandan: Well, even before the pandemic crisis that we are experiencing now, there was a radical shift towards online that forced businesses to pivot and those that didn't sadly lost out. It's really important for people to be able to embrace building that online relationship because that's where they're going to get found. That's where their customers are looking.

Oscar Calderon: So let's get down to brass tacks. How do we break it down? What's your process?

Mark Tandan: It is really simple. We want to find a way to make a customer feel special after they've ordered from us. There are two parts to that. I mean, it's one thing to make them feel special, but the real kicker is to do it as a surprise so they don't expect that it's coming. It's not like you lead with, "Hey, buy this and you'll get 10% off on your next order." The real trick that makes people remember you and feel like the experience was special is that there's a bit of a gift as a surprise. And that can be a lot of different things. I think you're going to probably want to know the specifics of what those are. So can I just transition into how that works? Give some examples?

Oscar Calderon: Yes, of course.

Mark Tandan: Awesome. Let's say you're selling anything online to an online consumer. You could simply just include a little bit of swag with whatever the deliverable is. For whatever reason, we don't outgrow stickers. Look at laptops and how they get smothered in stickers. This can also give you a bit of a branding opportunity. You could do a branded company coffee cup, a pen or a very low cost water bottle, which are all things that are going to gain you some exposure. Now that shouldn't really be the goal. The goal should be to make the customer think "Wow, I didn't expect that. That's really kind of cool." If you don't have any swag and you don't want to put anything into that, that's fine. Just a little coupon code for a discount on their next purchase will work. And the key here is to make that discount chunky enough that it's going to make them want to go shopping with you, even if they don't need anything at the time. So even if it costs you and it's going to cut into your margins, it's probably getting you a sale that you never had before. I'll give you a great example. There is a company called Brydge and they manufacture accessories for tablets, notably really cool keyboards for iPads and surfaces and things like that. I ordered one for a new iPad and I got a pretty good price. And right in the package was a little postcard with "Thanks for being a customer. Use this code for 20% off your next purchase with us." So I feel special. I'm surprised. And what do I do? I go on their website that afternoon, looking for what I am going to buy right then and there. This has a lot of different applications. It is going to increase customer value. Definitely. It's going to help with loyalty. Think of yourself. Have you ever gone to a restaurant and they just buy your dessert without even letting you know up front? They're just like, "Hey, dessert is on us tonight." And you just feel special. Has that ever happened to you, Ocar? You sort of get how that feels, right?

Oscar Calderon: Yeah.

Mark Tandan: So this is the same sort of thing, right? You're making the customer feel special. At the end of the day, they're either going to re-up right away with another order or they're going to hold you in higher regard. And the real bonus to this is it can even help with error recovery. For example, let's say you're new to online. You're transitioning to online and your checkout process isn't that smooth or your customer had a bit of a tricky time checking out. It was tough to navigate your website. Some stuff was out of your control and the customer wasn't really happy with the order process, but they're not mad enough to go ahead and complain. They're just probably not going to go to your website again. That's the worst case scenario. Then something like this hits them with their order... like a little freebie, a little bonus, a little incentive to come back. Not only is that great for them, but it also tends to override any negative emotion that they might have attached to that checkout experience.

Oscar Calderon: One hundred percent. I love it. And like you said, you create a goodwill at the same time, right? Psychologically, that sense of reciprocity when you get something, makes you want to give something.

Mark Tandan: Absolutely. And in this day of social media, people share these stories all the time. They like to share "feel good" stories. I'll tell anybody who listens that I think Timbuktu is the best gear company on the planet in terms of bike bags and travel stuff because they treat me like gold every single time. And you know, what a great way to build your brand...your customer becomes your ambassador.

Oscar Calderon: And one of the best parts is this is an asset that everyone has. Every business has that communication once the customer is buying something. And it is immediate. They have that deliverable in their hands so it is a perfect time to give something away, sell something else or create that sense of goodwill.

Mark Tandan: Yeah. For sure. You're cementing that relationship early. They found you and they overcame the biggest barrier right off the bat and bought from you. People are fickle and they'll look for the next best deal or the next best thing. But if you go in there and cement that relationship early, you stand a much better chance of them continuing to do business with you.

Oscar Calderon: Wow. Love it. I love it, Mark. If people want to know more about you and what you do, where can they find you?

Mark Tandan: The best way to go right now is on Facebook or LinkedIn. Just Mark Tandon. I live in Canada. So if you find a bunch of profiles, you won't find too many in Canada. So that's the easiest way to reach me.

Oscar Calderon: Awesome, Mark. Thank you for your time. We'll talk soon.

Mark Tandan: Thanks again, Oscar. All the best.

Mark Tandan

"You never win an argument with a prospective customer."

Ever since childhood, Mark Tandan has been fascinated by "using his words" to get others
to take very specific actions.

As a freelance copywriter, he's turned this fascination into tens of millions of dollars in
yearly sales for clients.

Mark likes blending both modern and classic copy principles, and doesn't believe that
hard & fast rules can be applied to every single product.

By going against the grain, he's had some animated arguments with clients ...
But he'll tell you that's part of the real fun of being a copywriter.

A former college instructor, Mark maintains a passion for teaching. With multiple
copywriting courses on Udemy and independent platforms, he stays connected with
thousands of fellow "conversion junkies".

Mark loves road cycling, logging hundreds of kilometers a week to compensate for his sedentary occupation … even if technically biking is still just sitting.

He also enjoys cooking and is even more experimental in the kitchen than he is with copywriting.

And to this day, he swears that the infomercial is one of the best examples of
direct response copywriting you'll ever see.

WEBSITE: www.click4more.ca

EMAIL: mark@click4more.ca

ABOUT THE PUBLISHER

Mark Imperial is a Best-Selling Author, Syndicated Business Columnist, Syndicated Radio Host, and internationally recognized Stage, Screen, and Radio Host of numerous business shows spotlighting leading experts, entrepreneurs, and business celebrities.

His passion is discovering noteworthy business owners, professionals, experts, and leaders who do great work, and sharing their stories and secrets to their success with the world on his syndicated radio program titled “Remarkable Radio”.

Mark is also the media marketing strategist and voice for some of the world's most famous brands. You can hear his voice over the airwaves weekly on Chicago radio and worldwide on iHeart Radio.

Mark is a Karate black belt, teaches kickboxing, loves Thai food, House Music, and his favorite TV shows are infomercials.

Learn more:
www.MarkImperial.com
www.ImperialAction.com
www.BooksGrowBusiness.com

www.ingramcontent.com/pod-product-compliance
Lightning Source LLC
LaVergne TN
LVHW020633100826
845148LV00012B/2176

* 9 7 8 1 7 3 2 3 7 6 3 7 3 *